# Christians, Where In Hell Are You?

## CAROLYN FRANKLIN M. A.

ISBN: 9781070256948
Imprint: Independently published

voicedynamicscf@yahoo.com

# Contents

# THE DECLINE IN CHRISTIAN CHURCH MEMBERSHIP

For some time in my readings I have come across articles and statistics of the decline in membership of established Christian churches. The trend seems to lead us to believe Christianity is on its way out with no dependable belief system to replace it.

Yet we have the seismic surge of Christians flooding the TV raconteurs. Why? What are these eloquent TV stars selling to bait the adoration, attendance and money from the small fish in a full net? What are these TV stars selling to the audience - other than a dazzling smile?

Watch the speakers, and listen. They are not selling "Christianity", they are selling personal growth, prosperity and self-aggrandizement - while blinding their listeners with a smile any orthodontist would give their sports cars for.

These TV hucksters are selling Hope, an easy Future free of stress and life's complications. They are selling Paradise today for only a few dollars down now, the rest to be paid in big installments - to the TV star. The more you donate, the more God will reward you.

However, there is one organized belief system that is growing exponentially, according to the statistics. That would be the Mormons. This is an independent organization from Christians. They, also, promise you a bright future in the Hereafter and the cost is flexible.

You have probably had a gaggle of beautiful blonde youngsters knock on your door, eager to share with you their memorized

1

patter. These youngsters are excited to talk with you. From the number of missionaries at large, it would seem the rise in their membership is impressive - people signing up by the hundreds or more.

But, before you sign up for a year's supply of toothpaste in anticipation of a financial windfall, check the stats on their birth rate, by far the highest in the nation, and other places. So, to increase membership stats and look good on paper, the solution is to breed, as fast as you can!

I met an older Mormon woman recently, her husband had just died. Between just the two of them they left 60 descendants. And these descendants are still of breeding age. That will help their membership.

One Mormon explained, "God told us to go forth and multiply." And I thought, "Yes, but multiply by the square root?"

And, just think, you and I get to pay their school taxes, library taxes, street lights, police/fire protection, sidewalks, rapid transit… Yes, the Mormons chip in, too - more kids!

But my question is, what are they doing, that would be <u>DO</u> - ING for others? For the inner cities?

But, this book is about the seeming steady decline and intensity of Christianity. Increasing attendance is not necessarily increasing "Christianity".

## MISSING IN ACTION

So, where are the Christians? If church membership is declining, and TV attendance is growing, that means there are no cohesive groups of people to do good works. There are scattered groups of

Christians that focus on caring for the homeless people, including families and children.

But there doesn't seem to be an organized, cohesive effort to demonstrate the purpose of Christianity, to spread the word, the teachings of Jesus and do what He did, go among the people who are lost and show them the path to Life.

## WHAT ARE YOU DO - ING?

And my basic question to Christians is what are you <u>DO</u> - ing for the disadvantaged, the homeless, the stoned, lost addicts, the child-gangs that roam the streets? DO - ing in an organized, *on-going* basis?

*When I was a single, working mother, my daughter was in a serious car accident where she had her leg amputated. The local Christian church offered to pay the hospital bill. I was deliriously grateful! They asked me to write a detailed letter about the accident. I thought that was odd, but I did it. The letter was submitted to a committee. A month went by. The Committee requested another letter with more detail about the accident. I sent another letter.*

*Another month went by. The Committee sent another request for more details. I was furious! Not only did I have her doctor's appointments, therapists appointments, prothesis appointments and my job to go to, but these letters were a constant reminder of the trauma we both suffered. I wrote the church a letter saying, "Send the damn money or leave me alone!" They did not send the damn money. They left me alone.*

*What were they do-ing?*

# CHRISTIANS, WHERE IN HELL ARE YOU?

Have you noticed the drive-by shootings, the school shootings, the random stabbings, wanton destruction of property, arson...the list never ends. And then we have these movements to ban guns. It's not the gun that's the problem - it's the shooter.

When I say that to my anti-gun friends, they look hard at me and very carefully explain, that guns kill people; if we get rid of guns, people will not be killed. Very simplistic, and true. But people who shoot others or wish others harm, will not be deterred by a lack of guns.

These people are ill, seriously mentally ill.

But, you say, "I'm not doing anything, I'm not ill - it's not my problem."

And that is exactly the problem, you're not do-ing anything! And "you" **are** the problem!

Oddly, I am not pro-gun. I am pro-mental health. The gun is only a symbol of a deeper illness, a sick society. Attend to the sick minds and guns will not be an issue.

Children are shooting children at schools. If we blame the shooting on the gun, then the parents are not responsible for their child having serious mental problems - it's society's problem - it's the gun, but not my son. The schools should have counseling centers. The teachers should be aware of problems - everyone but the parent "should do" something.

No parent wants the responsibility for their kids on drugs, vandalizing property, so it's societies' fault.

Today's society believes that kids are young, they need to express themselves freely and experience their personal life on their own

4

terms. The prevailing vacuous social trend is that children should be allowed to express themselves, experiment with their psyche, their intellect, their lives and the sanity of those around them.

Teaching responsibility will stunt their spiritual and intellectual growth. To impose beliefs that interfere with individual development is not the trend.

I asked one young mother if her daughter was going to Sunday School. They were not affiliated with any denomination, but it seemed to me to that have the child exposed to the ethics and teachings of Christianity was a part of a good education.

The mother replied, "We don't belong to a church. We're going to let her choose her own religion when she get older."

Choose, her own religion? From what? She has no idea what any of the basics are of the various denominations. It's like taking a two year old to the superstore and say, "OK, honey. What shall we have for dinner?" And let the child choose. Vacuous. Mind boggling. Stupid.

*Once, as a 6 year old, I announced to my mother that I would fix the dinner for that night. I bought jelly beans, all colors so we'd have a choice of flavors. I set the table and put a handful of the beans on each plate, quite pleased with myself.*

*Mother emptied the beans in the garbage and put food on the plates. I was annoyed but knew I better than to protest. I ate the food.*

## FREEDOM FROM RULES

Have you noticed the exponential disrespect for property, laws, the spread of drug abuse, drug sales…why should people obey laws when they're told they're entitled to freedom of expression?

How can we mete out justice when some law-breakers are "disadvantaged" and therefore untouchable? I mean, don't Christians see this disrespect as a sign of pervasive cultural sickness?

What are Christians doing about this "sickness"?

People are being profiled. They are profiled because these particular people are repeat offenders. But, society chooses to see it's not that they're breaking the law, they're being profiled - the police are unfair. The police tell someone to "put down their gun," they don't and they get shot. Maybe if they put down the gun, they wouldn't get shot.

Society has discovered that if people blame crime on circumstances, then no one is responsible. The high-risk population can't help drive-by shootings, can't help 7-11 robberies, stabbings on city transit buses, sidewalk robberies, gangs robbing merchants in broad daylight - no, these people are not responsible, they're disadvantaged.

If it weren't for the guns and the knives, the high crime rate would not exist. It's not my child, not my problem. Take the guns away and the problem will go away.

Crime is rampant. And it's getting worse.

Why?

Because the Christians don't care. Well, they do talk about it, form committees that review the situation, make reports and suggestions. This keeps them busy and can take a lot of time.

## HOW CHRISTIANS CARE

Oh, wait!

Yes, the Christians care - about gays - they condemn them! Gays are not going to heaven! They're sinners! Christians care about abortion. They're against abortions, but they don't seem to notice the glaring reason for abortion. Girls are impregnated by rape, raped and molested by family members and trusted friends. Only the girls who have had abortions will go to Hell. Their impregnators remain walking with their head held high - who me? It's not my fault! And the sin goes no farther. Incest and rape are sanctioned, shut behind the bedroom door.

Christians hold rallies against abortion. Christians meet on the sidewalks with banners, guitars, hand clapping to Christian songs while damning young girls who have no place to turn. Home is hell and the streets are worse. But the Christians assure these girls that "God loves them". Uhmmm, God does, but do Christians?

What are Christians doing about stopping of molesting children? Data shows both parents are involved. It's a well-kept secret. The Catholic church has been doing it for years. The Boy Scouts' leaders, gym teachers and cults are very slow getting stripped of their status.

Christians damn gays, who are people who harm no one, who just want to live a quiet life and be left in peace. So gays wear rainbow pajamas on the street; they wear their hair to please themselves. Who does that hurt? Gays aren't armed, they don't have drive-by's or shoot 7-11 clerks. And yet, God will punish them. For what?

Christ forgives, Christians damn.

What about the rampant drug use in young people, dying on the streets? What about young people committing suicide, the media pushing drugs and condoning habit-forming, mind-killing, soul-killing pills pushed by the slick, sexy sales people on TV and your local M. D.?

7

Where are the guitars, the banners, the hand-clappers and zealots when the opioid addicts are passed out on the sidewalks? Christians sing spirited songs about "Jesus loves you..." and walk around the bodies on the sidewalks.

I understand the libraries have a serious problem with drug addicts dying at libraries. The addicts can die quietly and undisturbed among the classic literature. Librarians keep a supply of NAM at their desk to revive these lost souls.

Scatology in TV programming? Filth is available at your convenience for all ages at all hours.

What are Christians doing about that?

Nothing.

I tried to get the Christians at my church to have a letter-writing campaign to sponsors of violent shows to boycott the programs and the congregation laughed at me.

It's called "free speech". Of course most TV's have an "off" switch, or a button on the remote - it's small, but it's there.

## MINISTERING TO THE INNER CITY

Meanwhile the inner city is a breeding ground for hatred, evil and self-destruction. It's a haven for the Anti Christ, the serpent of evil who preys on minds devoid of reason, wallowing in ignorance, devoid of the Light of Life. The Anti Christ grows strong in lies, deceit, the loss of ethics, of morals. It is an agent of greed, lies, corruption and deceit in government. American indulgence in evil is fertile soil for the Anti Christ.

The American inner cities are jungles of violence, where sundry forces are vigorously occupied in the destruction of souls. The evil is spreading exponentially to the neat suburbs causing people to move to safer areas.

Why don't the Christian missionaries "save" inner cities and bring Light to the lost? Are the beautiful blonde Christian missionaries afraid to face the inner city evil and "put on the whole armor of God" to vanquish it? Is the Anti Christ too powerful?

Forging missions in Detroit isn't exciting like saving natives in Kazakhstan, Ethiopia, Mongolia, Cambodia, Uganda, South Africa... Detroit doesn't have colorful native costumes that look great in selfies - well they do have torn sweat shirts as their costume de jour.

I'm not talking about individual people or groups who bring warm blankets for the homeless on a winter night. I'm not talking about people who serve a warm meal on a special holiday or once a day at a mission. I'm not talking about families that give up their Christmas celebration to bring presents for the homeless children. I'm not talking about my cousin who knit gloves for the homeless at winter, or the girl on the YouTube who gave her shoes and her warm coat to a homeless woman - on a winter afternoon.

I'm saying these acts should be commonplace, done as a general expectation. Acts of benevolence, of kindness, of sharing by Christians should be as commonplace as driving on the right side of the road.

Why did God send His son to earth... To save us from what? Our own ignorance and naïveté? The Anti Christ is breathing down our necks even in the houses of worship, and we welcome it in with open arms. We call it "freedom of religion". The Anti Christ teaches "soul-icide", an attack on the concept of Life Everlasting as taught by the Bible.

Rather than examine their off-center beliefs, some Christians retaliate criticism by stating, " My church is the 'one, true' church." We have the "one, true god". Does God know that? Is that church named in the Bible? This belief is the height of ignorance.

*I have just read, "Coming Clean" an autography of Jorge Valdes, a drug runner for the Medellin Drug Cartel here in America. He would fly his plane to various third world countries to pick up a cargo of cocaine to sell in America. While there he would give money to the people who were hungry and homeless. Several times he paid off peoples' mortgages and gave money for food. He said what annoyed him was that the people in these countries were very poor, hungry and homeless and the priest would go among them asking for donations rather than take care of their needs.*

Jorge had a hard childhood in Cuba where he felt that God had forsaken him. When he saw the destitute people in third world countries with the priest expecting money, Jorge was convinced there was no God. If there were a God, these people would not be suffering.

I never could understand how you can take donations from the poor to give to the poor…?

Wake up, Christians, the night is coming! Send missionaries to clean up the American inner cities, bring in the Light! The destructive forces breeding in the inner cities are a direct challenge to the Christian way of life. We must stand *united*!

Our Preamble to the Constitution sets the stage for who Americans should be, who and what we built this country for.

# PREAMBLE TO THE CONSTITUTION OF THE UNITED STATES

"We the People of the United States, in Order to form a more perfect Union, establish Justice, insure domestic Tranquility, provide for the common defence, promote the general Welfare, and secure the Blessings of Liberty to ourselves and our Posterity, do ordain and establish this Constitution for the United States of America."

Have you read this document lately, at all? Ever? Do you know what it is? It's an attention-getter, commonly called, "**The Preamble** to the Constitution of the United States." It sums up the reason for writing our Constitution.

It says we have a Constitution to ensure the States are united to establish justice, promote peace, unite in "defence," promote the general welfare and maintain freedom for ourselves and prosperity.

A noble endeavor, for a unique country, the only one of its kind, ever. And, it's ours, AMERICA!

So, at this point in our nation, what have we done to "insure domestic tranquillity"?

What is our "common" defense?

How have we promoted "peace"?

How have we promoted general welfare?

Go on to the next page for answers.

**PROMOTING "PEACE"**

**BOOM!! BOOM! BOOM!!....,...BOOMBOOMBOOM!!
....... Hahahaha...**

The noise was deafening.

The boys were sprawled on the floor laughing loudly in triumph, playing games on TV. They each held some kind of box with their thumbs pressed intently on control buttons while their eyes focused on the flashing screen.

Elongated robots with hinged elbows and knees thundered across the screen, their monster feet crushing civilization as we know it. Fragments of human bodies dropped from their mouths - slits in a bug-shaped head. Blasts of white, red and black smoke, shrapnel, bullets, bombs blew up the city.

The noise was deafening. Every bomb blast ripped through my ears, my mind and my soul. The boys were having fun, laughing and swinging the controls as they blew up a monster chewing the militia. Frantic, minuscule humans were scattered on the TV screen, scrambling for safety.

**"WOW!! DIDJA SEE THAT?" Hahahaha....**

Conversation was impossible.

Thinking was impossible.

Intelligence was impossible.

And, I think that's the point.

# BRAIN POISON

"Thinking" is less and less an issue in today's world. We follow, and swallow the idiocy on media. People vote for idiots based on what they say, not what they do. Political assurances are meaningless patter concocted to delude the listener. Politicians will expound on what they think we want to hear.

Almost without exception, politicians are million, billion - aires. How did they get so rich? All of them - so rich. Did get good pay for bagging at the supermarket? Selling magazines? Do you think these billionaires really give a thought to you?

Amassing our votes is a gateway to vast reservoirs of taxes, loopholes, free jet rides, trip to Monaco to visit the "poor"…?

Polls are taken, trends are examined and then candidates base their speeches on what sells, not necessarily what's the best direction for the people.

Ask Google. Pray to Google. Google knows all.

Some years ago as TV progressed to a choice of more stations and less blur and static on the screen, I began to notice a leaning toward violence in programming. "Leave It To Beaver," "The Donna Reed Show" and "Burns and Allen" were slowly usurped by "Dragnet," "The Untouchables" and "Maverick".

Those "action" programs were mild compared to today. Now it gets much worse. The transition from family humor to bloody bodies was slow, but steady - relentless. Today programs for the general public at accessible hours rely on gratuitous violence for entertainment. The erosion from mild murder mysteries to wanton bloodshed has-been slow, but steady. Today we're inured to the the damage they do to our mind, to our psyche.

PBS programming has "murder" programs but the bodies were always rather tastefully arranged. No blood stains splattered across the walls, no scenes of gruesome headless corpses - innuendo, yes, but no body parts. That's a help.

Some time ago, a man whom I greatly admire, Steve Allen, a musician, comedian and philosopher, stated "TV was sewage." I now realize the depth of his vision. And we invite this "sewage" into our home almost all day every day.

At this time we have sacrificed quality in programming to pander to pointless, low class violence. It seems each program is trying to outdo the other for credit ratings in bad taste, resulting in unadulterated, saliva-dripping violence.

Is there a goal in mind with this blood-spattered entertainment?

I saw the trend toward violence developing one inch at a time. The trend was clear to me, that someone, some group, was focused on getting the public to absorb superfluous evil - encouraging us to see pain and destruction as entertainment. Cartoons were based on destruction of life and property.

I mean, where's the harm? It's only cartoons; it's not real. It won't affect real life nor damage anyone in real life - it's just a show.

Some time ago family interaction on TV programming was an example of family cohesion. The father was the head of the family, the mother handled domestic tasks and the children had activities that were constructive and cooperative.

The family programming today is adversary interaction, constant arguing, one-upmanship: "Roseanne", "Modern Family", "The Goldbergs", "Raymond", "Mash"… You get the idea.

Where are the Christian values of helping each other, listening to each other, speaking reasonably politely to everyone? Has it gone out of style? What are Christians thinking when they tune in these vacuous programs? Do we have standards any more about civility?

*Recently on my neighborhood watch link, there was a short video of a neighbor, in walking his dog, and the dog accidentally knocked over the mail box. The owner of the mailbox was annoyed because the person didn't stop for a moment and say the box was down. That would have been a courtesy.*

*The response of the other neighborhood link-watchers was, "Well the box was old anyway. You should put up a new one." The concept of "courtesy" was completely out of anyone's mind! It was not the box the owner was concerned about - it was courtesy!*

## IT'S OK, THE PSYCHOLOGISTS HAVE SAID SO

Psychologists have studied the trend toward mayhem and have concluded that focusing hour after hour of destruction, loud noise and lifeless human bodies is harmless.

And then the evening news reflects the same violence on the streets that we saw in the "entertainment". Who can separate reality from the hypnotizing drama we "enjoy" on the TV?

As a child I, intensely disliked Popeye, Road Runner, The Three Stooges - all gratuitous violence. Popeye was bullied by Brutus. They would beat each other up and it only stopped when Popeye swallowed some spinach.

Then Popeye pummeled Brutus.

Is that funny?

Laurel and Hardy were very popular, gentle and funny. They were kind to each other and all the characters on the screen. I think that kindness would go over big today. What programs today feature "kindness"?

Amos and Andy, my favorite radio program as a child. It was about two old friends, Black men, who put up with their wives in a very gentle way. They had a calm, philosophical approach to life and commented on the things that made no sense, but didn't try to change the world.

They were White men playing the part of Black men. Suddenly it was "racist," and taken off the air. It was a kind, gentle program and was greatly missed. They were the "Mr. Rogers" of radio.

I am confused. There is a Hollywood production of "Snow White" played by a Black girl and… that's ok…? Can you have it both ways?

When I was in college in the '70's there was a class on campus of old time comedy shows, Laurel and Hardy (my favorites), Harold Lloyd, Buster Keaton, W.C. Fields, Abbott and Costello, all innocent comedy, clean, funny and wholesome.

The films were shown in a classroom, but also, students could stand outside and look in through the windows. The crowd outside was 3 people deep and everyone laughing! It made me so happy to see all kinds of people enjoying light-hearted comedy, Black Panthers, nerds, hippies, Nervous Nellies, all together, laughing and liking each other. Hatred was forgotten for an hour or so.

Good, clean, gentle humor is never out of date. People saying, "Excuse me, thank you, please," is never out of date.

However, "good, clean humor" doesn't seem to sell today. Many of the TV programs seem to be based on wanton sex, wanton, gratuitous violence. The scripts are easy to follow as the major word is the "F" word, over and over. That takes little talent and imagination to write and for the actor to memorize.

Americans are wading knee deep in muck and sinking further down. Scatology is cheap and easy to write. But the results are that this level of intelligence and performance reduce the quality of life and respect for self and others.

Don't let violence take over our lives and our minds! People emulate behavior - they copy what they see - they see violent behavior as exciting and destructive. They don't understand that by encouraging violent behavior it will come into their homes and destroy them - not just on TV!

Christians need to band together as one united force to stop this encroaching evil. We know that this beautiful country is a gift of God. The destiny of America is meant to be a sanctuary from the very forces that invade us today.

America was not meant to be a country where death, destruction and fear surround the people. But, we are sliding fast to a place of no return. We are destroying ourselves and only the force of Christianity can stop it.

It's never too late or too "old fashioned" to stop evil, and only Christians can do it. Why do we allow this corruption of the minds of the children and young adults? They certainly are not capable of choosing healthy programming, there's none to choose from! With the demise of Mr. Rogers, much of the healthy, constructive TV for children is gone.

So, full of confidence in the intelligence of Christians, I made an announcement at church, "It's obvious TV programing is pandering to the lower-class minds. The content is fast-growing in violence and killings. I suggest we have a letter-writing campaign to the sponsors and tell them we won't buy their products until the violence in programming is stopped."

They laughed. The Christians laughed!

I was stunned and disappointed. If Christians don't stop violence, who will? If Christians don't follow the 10 Commandments, who will?

Well, so far, it seems very few people, even Christians - well, not enough "Christians " are either following the 10 Commandments or demonstrating the words of Jesus.

In fact, Christians are embarrassingly indifferent to the mental poison on TV, films, computer media, individual communication systems, email, texting and current books (I say "books" rather than "literature" as I feel the two concepts are on separate levels of intelligence.)

Christians have lost their way; we are lost in a hall of mirrors, our vision is blocked by false reflections.

# THE FIRST AMENDMENT "FREE" SPEECH

We explain our inability to stop TV violence because of the First Amendment; we allow the integrity of our minds and belief systems to be violated - it's free speech. True. But we can speak louder by boycotting the TV stations, the products and the sponsors. We can write letters and email companies our displeasure. We have the "freedom" to choose to buy or not to buy.

Many times I have written to companies when I felt there was a social problem that needed attention, changing or updating.

In every case they listened and usually made changes. Some companies even called me and others wrote a letter. Companies want to hear from you - you're the one that pays the CEO's wages!

Some psychologists have concluded TV has no impact on the mind, no influence.

Utter nonsense!

Who pays them for that vacuous conclusion? Use your own intelligence! You don't need a PhD when you see something that is unproductive and damaging to young minds. Use your head! Use your common sense! Use the U.S. Mail!

My experience in the social sciences is that very few people use common sense - even in the upper education levels. Just because

Dr. So and So says something doesn't mean it's credible. Use your own common sense.

Is encouraging suicide free speech? Is unplugging the rot on the internet a denial of free speech? A denial of "rights?" Do parents have any power to "parent" any more?

At one major New York museum there was a display, a portrait, of the Madonna, Mary, the Mother of Jesus. Instead of oils, acrylic, water colors or pencil, the portrait was done in cow manure.

Yes, cow manure.

I was horrified, outraged and furious.

And what did the Christians do?

Nothing.

*Nothing.*

## *NOTHING!*

It's called, "free speech," and I understand that. But the museum is a big business and we can walk with our voices, our feet and our email. We, Christians, have free speech, too.

What would Muslims do if their faith had been so insulted?

# "FREE SPEECH": A TWO-EDGED SWORD

Art, as such, is a "speech." People can paint what they want in what media they want. They have every legal right to express their feelings about the Mother of Jesus, the Son of God. Insulting her is just a way of "self" expression, self reflection - "art."

Christians don't see how depicting the Mother of God by manure is a representation of self-loathing, self humiliation, of *our self,* the slide of American pride into a "waste" land of lost people who walk in darkness heading for a bottomless pit.

On the other hand, Christians can write letters of protest, walk in front of the museum with placards, write letters to the Museum leaders, write to the radio stations - our feet, our pen, our voices are all tools - weapons of the First Amendment.

I mentioned this situation to several of my Christian friends, and not one seemed perturbed. Some of them laughed and walked away.

This "laughter," in the face of violating the very core of Christianity, is a reflection of our self-respect - we have almost none. And, we're doing it to ourselves.

In Joan Rivers' book, "Still Talking," she says:

*When I listen to Andrew Dice Clay, I marvel that I ever thought Dick was a proper name and blow is what you do to balloons. Sam Kinison insults everybody - including AID sufferers and Kurds who were killed by parachuted food supplies.He says all*

21

*old people should be put to death after eighty five, and brought a crippled dwarf onstage to call Jerry Lewis a son of a bitch. He insults Christians. Kinison pounds on the floor and shouts Christ's last words, "OUCH! OUCH!" He's outrageous but brilliant.*

He's "brilliant?", or is he full of hate, perhaps jealous of the richness - the beauty, of Christianity; Jesus, the Son who brought us hope and gentleness. Comedy is often a way to express anger, bitterness and emptiness.

And, we think that's funny - in fact, "brilliant"!! We feel if everyone says it's funny and we don't laugh, there's something wrong with us. The man is crying for help, and we laugh.

We Christians go to these performances and pay people to insult the Son of God.

But the degrading message of Clay is not new. The public is just more accepting. Comedy, "humor", often performed on the brink of cruelty, is sinking deeper into darkness and we're going along for the ride.

## CHRISTMAS

There are those Christians who don't celebrate the birthday of Jesus. They say it's a pagan holiday.

NO, it's not!

We are observing the *birth* of the Son of God. **THE *SON OF GOD***! We don't need a tree, we don't need the lights - it's **His BIRTH** we're celebrating - not the day! We are **NOT** celebrating December 25! We are **NOT** celebrating jingle bells on a one-horse open sleigh...

Of course Christmas, the birth-day of Jesus, is not in the Old Testament - *he wasn't born yet!*!

Who cares what *day* it is! There is something wrong with the shallow thinking of those people, "Christians," who erroneously celebrate the *day,* and not the *event.*

Think about the Day as described in the New Testament. Three Kings left on a long, arduous journey with a brilliant, huge Star to guide them. It took weeks to find the Baby, but the star led them there, shining the whole time.

When He was born, angels came down from heaven and sang to the shepherds and everyone present, "Fear not! For behold, I bring you good tidings of great joy, which shall be unto **ALL PEOPLE.** For unto you is born this day in the city of David, a Savior which is Christ the Lord..."

The Three Kings arrived with their wonderful gifts.

It was quite an observance! The immense star dominating the sky, shining over the world for all to see - the Three Kings in their gorgeous robes, the shepherds huddled together, "quaking at the sight," the sky filled with the brightness, the beauty of thousands of angels singing, "Rejoice... fear not! For He has come...the Savior of Mankind!"

It was a celebration! They were celebrating a birthday!

Hey! - Somebody put on a helluva show for our benefit!

Is God telling us something? It seems God wants our attention...

Is God a pagan?

# THE "POOR" BABE

One of the on-going myths about the birth of Jesus is that Joseph was "poor." Jesus was born in a manger because Joseph had no money to get a suite at the Bethlehem Hilton.

Joseph was a capitalist, he owned a construction business; he was a master carpenter, and Mary, his wife, was from a respectable family of good lineage. As such she wouldn't do her own housework or the laundry. She very likely had servants to take care of her needs.

So, why was the Baby born in a manger? Well, Joseph and Mary tried several hotels, but there were no vacant rooms. The only space left was in the stable with all the animals - but, for a woman close to giving birth, any place to rest is welcome.

After all, she just made a long trip , 90 miles, riding side-saddle on the back of a donkey. Just thinking about that makes my back hurt - really hurt!

A stable is a ground-level location, probably no door, wide open to let the various animals pass in and out easily. So, after the baby was born, *everyone* had access to Him, the shepherds, the animals, the kings - there was room for *everyone*, and *everyone, and every thing* was welcome - they were all on the same level.

If He had been born in the Hilton, Room 3310, the Presidential Suite, everyone - especially the goats and the sheep, would have been banned from entering. That was not the Plan.

Today, this separation of God's people, into denominations, is pathetic. Each one announces it is the "true" church, the only way to reach God. Actually, in a way, this is blasphemy; God did not intend us to separate into competing groups of worshippers, each implying it is God's favorite.

24

God doesn't like that.

## CHRISTMAS CARDS

If you choose to send out cards to celebrate His birth, Christians, why are you sending cute ducks in red pajamas? Why are you sending cards with puppies in Santa suits, deer posing among shimmering pine trees in the glittering dusk of a winter night, churches with snow covered steeples and windows with glowing, golden lights? Or, happy children sledding down a mound of snow? Happy teens ice skating on a sparkling frozen lake....?

Or, a card to your mother-in-law that says something like, "You look like the donkey standing next to the manger - except he weighs less!"

If you're going to send out Christmas cards, then send out cards that express the JOY of HIS BIRTH! That one sacred moment that changed the course of mankind!

It's a shame that some "Christians" have a soul so bereft of joy, good will and beauty that they try to diminish the joy others experience uplifted from that life-changing gift.

## HERB CAEN - SAN FRANCISCO CHRONICLE

Herb Caen was a popular columnist for many years at the San Francisco Chronicle. He was a Jew, and on occasion alluded to that fact.

For many years now, Christians have admonished other Christians not to say "Merry Christmas" to people as we might offend them.

**OFFEND** them!!!

Herb Caen was annoyed about that. He said, "I'm a Jew, but if someone wishes me a 'Merry Christmas,' I'll take it! Any time someone wishes me well, I'll take it!"

I was so grateful to him for saying that. This is a land of free speech. Christians can say, "Merry Christmas," if they want to - to anyone they want to. If someone is offended and doesn't like it, well, *I'm offended* that they're offended!

How dare someone take offense at a gesture of Love, a gesture of good will? What about *my* getting offended?

Why is it only Christians are supposed to be careful not to offend someone? It works both ways.

At my church we were expecting a group of Jews to visit, sort of a "hands across the aisle" idea. Our priest was very nervous at the thought of having Jews at our service. She gathered us together and gave explicit instructions we were not to mention the name of Jesus, as it might offend them.

What..........?

We were apologizing for being Christians, in our own church! The enormity of that stupidity staggered my mind and I have never gotten over it.

> *Because I am very interested in religions, people's beliefs and their customs, I joined a Jewish choir at a synagogue in San Francisco.*
>
> *I sang with them for 4 years and found that they have an unwavering belief in themselves. They support each other and are alert for any perceived misunderstanding in their beliefs.*

*In order to respect their self-perception, I asked the Rabbi, "Do you prefer to be called, 'Jews' or 'Jewish'?"*

*He said, "I'll speak on that tonight."*

*What he said was, "The suffix, 'ish' means to be sort of something, 'It's 6-ish,' not quite six o'clock yet, but close. The color is 'red-ish' not quite red, but close.*

*We are JEWS, not 'Jew-ish' - we are not 'sort of Jews,' we are JEWS."*

How I admire that unwavering faith in their identity - there is no doubt in their mind about who they are, their past, their goals and their future direction.

We Christians have much to learn from the Jews.

Ask someone, "Are you a Christian?" And they may reply, "I'm a Presbyterian."

What does that tell you?

## CHRISTMAS STAMPS

The postal stamp depicting Christian art work is an outward statement of faith, an affirmation of our joy at the birth of the Son of God.

If you're so bold as to send out Christmas cards and you're not concerned with offending anyone, then go whole hog and use the stamps with the Christmas scene on it. Those stamps are specially made for the occasion and they don't cost extra.

# EASTER

For Christians this is probably the most sacred day of Christ's life. He died and he said he would return - he did. Again, what difference does it make what the day is? He rose from the dead - the ultimate in miracles.

And yet some Christians choose to ignore the day! It is such an insult to the Prince of Peace and our Creator not to at least hold a special day of Thanks for giving His life for us; He paid the ransom for our freedom.

This ignorance is a blatant insult!

Using your power and gift of free speech to uphold the practice of Christianity. This will strengthen the practice of decency in America. We need to revive the desire to follow the teachings of Jesus. And, we need to re-install the desire for ethics in the world around us out of self-respect.

## THE TEACHINGS OF JESUS

My cousin, Steve, was a student at the Mid America Baptist Theological Seminary, intending to earn his Bachelor of Divinity. On weekend evenings for fun and extra income, he played blue grass music on his banjo, guitar or fiddle at a local inn at the town center.

The head of the school told him to stop playing music there as the people were heathens, they drank, smoked and, in general, lived a godless life, a life of sinners.

Steve wondered, where in the Bible does Jesus say it's a sin to drink, smoke and listen to blue-grass?

It doesn't. He left the seminary.

To be a *"Christ* - ian" means to follow Jesus, the "CHRIST". The word, "christ" means, "Master", "Teacher", "Rabbi" - the man in charge. The correct title of Jesus should be, "Jesus, the Christ".

> As it says in Math 6:24: *"No man can serve two masters: for either he will hate the one, and love the other; or else he will hold to the one and despise the other. You cannot serve God and mammon.*
>
> *Matthew 3:16 - 17: and a voice came from heaven saying, "This is my son in whom I am well pleased."*
>
> *John 3:16: for God so loved the world that He gave His only begotten Son that whosoever believeth in Him should not perish but have everlasting life.*

These words, describing Jesus, are from the Gospel, the four books in the New Testament. You can either follow this teaching in the New Testament or wander far afield in the Old Testament.

These words from the New Testament are to convince us Jesus is God, the Father. Not a representative.

Jesus - IS GOD!

Therefore, the teachings, the words of Jesus are directly from God.

## So, What, Specifically, Did Jesus Teach?

At the request of His mother, He changed water into wine. So, I guess wine is ok...? I asked one Fundamentalist about that, and she said, "They mean He turned the water into grape juice."

If the translation is so wrong in one case, how many other places is the translation wrong? That's a huge discrepancy.

He told the prostitute to "go and sin no more". So I guess that means she will not go to Hell; she is forgiven. He didn't say prostitution is a sin, but I wonder if using your body in a way that humiliates it, is the sin?

Does the customer have any part in her "sin"? Does he ever repent?

I have never heard a pastor, or Christian, condemn the customer of a prostitute.

Why not?

Jesus said to pray in secret and give alms in secret (which the Muslims do). He said God knows what we're doing and we'll get points for that.

Working on the Sabbath or having fun on that day is no problem. According to Jesus, he said the Sabbath was made for man, not man for the Sabbath.

Jesus condemned the money makers in the temple. That was not the purpose of God's house.

Jesus' **one commandment** was:

*Love God above all things
and treat your neighbor the way you'd like him to treat you.*

That's it.

Jesus did not condemn us, He loved us. He understood us. He treated us the way the taught us to treat others with more patience and understanding.

Jesus knew we were human, and as such we are prone to make mistakes in our behavior and in our judgement of our self and others.

The purpose of His death, the drama, the injustice of it, His suffering, His unimaginable pain and humiliation, was to impress upon us humans the depth of His Love for us.

The Old Testament is not *Christian* teachings. It's a history book instilling in us the fear of damnation, retribution; it explains incest, carnal desires, lust, drunkenness, murder - in short - sensationalism, a tabloid on dried goat skin.

It did give us the Ten Commandments, which, I personally feel, are a very good idea.

## HUMAN ALL TOO HUMAN

On reflecting Nietzsche's observation that we are "all too human", we find we make a great many mis-takes. Is there enough time to reflect on and excuse the mis-takes - the sins - we make as humans?

Do we give ourselves any latitude for error, room to learn, to regret, to grow? Do we give others any latitude for error, room to learn, to regret, to grow?

### Judge Not Lest Ye Be Judged?

This does not mean "Judge not lest ye be judged", it means to teach people to treat each other with respect. But, we don't judge the person. We judge the behavior; we need to change the behavior. We must teach people acceptable social behavior - that is "judging".

We cannot turn people loose, to do whatever feels good. But, rather than condemn them, we need to teach them. We need to teach responsibility for one's actions, one's choice of behavior.

This "teaching" starts at childhood. Every child born must be a "wanted" child, a child born out of love and the understanding of the task of being responsible for a baby. We cannot allow "girls" to have babies. We cannot allow children to be birthing children.

Children are not mature, so cannot understand the burden, the responsibility of another life. Children cannot control their own life, how can they be responsible for others? If we are *Christ*-ians, it is our duty to teach responsibility for our own actions.

The "sin" is ours, we Christ-ians. We are responsible adults and when we allow children to have children, each Christ-ian is responsible. We know better, yet we turn our head to the side. If we don't "see" the sin, it doesn't exist.

Welfare encourages children to have children. Welfare pays children to have children. It is our task as Christians to teach the seriousness of bringing a new life into this world and have each potential mother understand the ramifications of that responsibility. Babies should be born only to responsible parents (plural).

# FREE WILL

Abandon all hope all ye who enter here - but, what if they've never had hope - like people in the inner city?

What if they have no "mind"? They're crazy…?

Allah - it's the will of Allah. Muslims believe all that happens is the will of Allah. Someone gets up in the morning, straps on a bomb and then says, "Today I'm going to kill non-believers…"

How is that the WILL of Allah? How can *you decide* to do something, and blame it on someone else? - on God?

Karma says…..it's all up to you… there's a price to pay for anything you do - or, think.

Christians say, "It's the will of God." Is it? Are you sure?

Yes, we have free will, we make choices. But…the Bible says, "*Ask*, and it will be given unto you."

That is "*YOU*" do the asking - when and if, YOU'RE ready. You are NOT under orders, - a commandment. This *order* to ask implies free will; it implies choice.

People who rob 7-11's and carry a gun, people who sell drugs and destroy other people's minds, people who walk away from their children and leave them to society to care for, people who mug the homeless, who bully kids, who ruin art works with Graffiti, do so of their own accord - their own free will.

People who destroy human lives in the inner city and beyond because they want money, revenge or malice, *do so because they want to.*

Yes, it might be because no one loves them, they've been abandoned, it's the way they survive - there are many reasons why people are destructive.

*But, ultimately, they do it out of their own free will.*

And, here you have a segment of the population who will say, "Not necessarily - they're disadvantaged."

All right, let's look at that. They are disadvantaged. That's a legitimate description.

Let's say there are two kinds of destructive people in society, first those people who willfully destroy and secondly, those people who destroy and have no understanding of the damage they do.

My question is, "Why?" If Christians perceive some behaviors as destructive, why do we allow it?

Why does a Christian society allow these people to continue the destruction? People who hate, destroy out of malice and also those people who are mentally warped, ill, lost?

They exist because we, Christians, allow them to exist.

We know there are damaged people, people who suffer from mental disease or anguish, people in need of physical care, people in need of a kind word.

So, we pray for them.

That's what we do for the lost people, we pray for them. We have a potluck dinner, lots of uplifting songs with guitars where we clap and dance and pray for the needy. We take up a collection for the needy. We smile a lot. All is well.

We hand the money to someone and then we go home and watch TV. Usually we have our favorite shows, where people are wantonly slaughtered but it's all resolved in 60 minutes. Not to worry.

# PARENTING

Esther Wojcicki, mother of 3 "powerful," girls has been touted on TV for having raised successful daughters. Two of her daughters are CEO's and one is a PhD.

(By the way, "powerful" is the new buzz word to describe the affluent.)

That's wonderful. Mrs. Wojcicki says she raised her daughters to be successful on the concepts of respect, trust, autonomy and individuality. I wonder if they are also provided with birth control.

She doesn't mention that both she and her husband have a handsome income, so can provide the luxuries of elite schools for their children as well as the respect and trust that comes with privilege. Her children are protected and cared for.

For children to be "successful" it helps to have a mother *and* father, an intact home in the suburbs, a 6 figure salary, and access to the school of your choice. It's less of a challenge to raise successful children when you have everything to give them to help them get started.

Success, borne out of affluence, is not "free will" - *it's destiny.*

In the inner city there is no "parenting." Girls have children and the children grow up - or they don't. If one or two - or three girls get lost lost in the shuffle, no matter, others will take their place.

Instead of assuming responsibility for fatherless, home-less children, instead of adopting them, it's easier for society to feel sorry for them and give a handsome donation to buy off any odd pangs of conscience.

We Christians will send money and prayers, then go out for tennis, then lunch at "Andre's."

Maybe we'll even discuss how we could provide these girls with information on birth control..., uh, no. That's not God's will. Their pregnancy is the result of their life style - in this case we can't interfere with their "free" will.

One Harvard student told me that these girls can have as many babies as they want. I thought that was magnanimous since as a Harvard student she didn't work and pay taxes. Her daddy did that.

Pregnancy could possibly be the result of ignorance..? Maybe we should send these inner-city girls to Harvard - then they can choose birth control!

## PARENTING - LET THE CHILDREN LEARN BY EXPERIENCE

I was shopping in one of those "warehouse" type superstores. At the moment I was seated at the coffee section resting and I happened to see a mother with two children in tow. The boy, about 4, was beating his sister with his fists, incessantly beating on her. The girl, about 6, was drowning in tears and cries. She put up her hands to defend herself to no avail.

36

I looked at the mother, she was looking at the hot dog relishes, fully concentrating on which mustard to use.

I went up to her angry, and stated, "That boy has been beating on this little girl non-stop. Why do you allow that?"

She didn't reply, but bent down, tipped her head and spoke some soft, sweet words to the boy. He paid her absolutely no attention.

I went home, called the police non-emergency number to ask for guidance. I wanted to ask about reporting child abuse. The officer said to get the license of their car, and the police would report the matter to the DHS (Department of Human Services). So, if I see this again, I will report it.

I mentioned this incident on our neighborhood talk link and the responses I got knocked me over! One woman was outraged! She said, "That is the most judgmental thing I have ever heard! You don't know what their circumstances were - you don't know the kind of day the mother was having! You shouldn't judge others!"

What I understood her message to be was, "Never mind if a little girl was being beat up - it's not your business!"

What would Jesus say - to the woman at the well, the woman being stoned, was He judgmental?

Is this the direction of today's "Christianity"?... none of my business...

# MORE ON CHRISTIAN MISSIONARIES

## DOUBLE THINK

Probably, the LDS, Mormons, are the epitome of energy for recruiting new members to their organization.

The young, healthy, beautiful people who knock at your door and smile when you meet them are sincere about wanting you to join them in their spiritual journey.

In their talk to convert you, they fail to mention they're not actually "Christians," they're Jews - well, not orthodox Jews, sort of ad hoc Jews. The Book of Mormon specifically states they are the lost tribe of Israel which predates the advent of Jesus, the Christ.

In fact, for some period of time, the Mormons were "baptizing" Jews after the Jews had died. The Mormons would take the names, from the obituaries, of Jews who had died and baptize them into the Mormon belief system.

The Jews were outraged and told the Mormons to stop it.

The Mormons stopped it - well, they said they did.

In the Book of Mormon there is no specific mention of the birth of Jesus, the life of Jesus and His specific teachings. When I took the indoctrination lessons to help people learn about Mormons, I asked this specific question:

"Do Mormons understand Jesus to be the son of God, the Only begotten Son of God?"

This belief is primary to real Christians. We base our entire belief of God on this one concept.

So, what was the answer the Mormon teacher told me...? She squirmed for a moment, I assume to form the best answer. Then she said, "He was one of the prophets. There are many prophets. Joseph Smith was a prophet, too..."

Joseph Smith and Jesus are the only Son of God...?

At this time the Mormons have erected a large building in Jerusalem, a school. The news says the Jews are concerned the Mormons will proselytize for members in the Holy City. The Mormons promise they won't. We may see a holy war over this! My money's on the Jews!

The LDS can trap two disparate major religions at once - even if they do cancel themselves out. How can you believe the Messiah "has/has not" come?

When in doubt, READ their literature, open your eyes. Read ALL religious literature to be fully informed. But not only literature from that belief system, read opposing views. That's called "education".

It comes down to a clever scheme of marketing for profit and increase membership - you get a two-for-one deal, your lineage and salvation are secure. In the general American capitalistic system, it's easier to sell Jesus than Judaism.

It may seem as though I am distressed with one belief system over the others. Not really. I intensely dislike it when anyone pretends to be something they're not. This includes Christians who are not followers of Jesus. Many are followers of a TV god.

# VENEZUELA, COLUMBIA, AFGHANISTAN...AFRICA

These are but a drop in the ocean of places America helps, either with money, education, health care and missionary work. All good deeds, and rightly so.

Americans see these countries as exotic, exciting, interesting. Just think how much fun it is to go there and save the natives. The missionaries take pictures in native costumes, some are holding adorable native babies swaddled in brightly died robes or the missionaries are surrounded by native children all looking up at the camera, smiling in the bright sun - on cue.

After a year or so of dedicated service, the missionaries return home to the acclamations of the congregation. They return to their home church and tell spellbinding tales of digging wells for clean water, planting rows of nutritious crops to show the natives how to eat properly for a good, balanced diet.

The congregation is spell-bound at the successes and tales of how the missionaries overcame floods, disease and rebel armies. The congregation knows their money was well-spent converting the heathens.

On the news I recently saw a group of tall, blond, young missionaries teaching Africans, who wore colorful native straw skirts, how to choreograph and sing some bright American song. Everybody was smiling. The opportunity for selfies was infinite.

Do they know that song in Detroit?

Are there heathens in Detroit? What about Birmingham? Memphis, Oakland - are there heathens there? Do we send in bus loads of fresh-faced youngsters to save the "downtrodden," "depressed," "disadvantaged," "lost" people in the cement jungle?

Do we go in to explain their rights? Their wrongs? Do we teach them to read, write and, think ? Do we explain to them how to live in peace with the tribes outside their 'hood? - outside their "turf"? Do we show them how to enjoy a balanced diet? I read somewhere that many people in those areas live on fried calories only, no fresh fruit, green vegetables or balanced meals.

These natives need to be saved.

# INNER CITY
# MISSIONARIES

For many of us, the "inner" city is a foreign land. How many of us reading this book have ventured into the recesses of our city which are known as "high crime" areas?

*One night I had been at a meeting and when I left, I stopped at a rather large grocery store in a nice location. It was park-like and had plenty of light.*

*I bought some things and, when I returned to my car, a skinny Black kid came up and slashed my head 3 times with a box knife.*

*Not one to run in fear, I grabbed the kid and his jacket ripped apart in my hands. He ran off and I ran into near-by fast food place, dripping blood from my head and saying, "Call the police - I've just been cut by a Black kid!"*

*A Black kid working at the counter walked away, making it obvious he didn't care. A Chinese kid working there immediately got on the phone and called 911. By now I was hysterical.*

*When the officers got there, they rushed me to the hospital. On the ride there, an older Black officer put his arms around me and held me tight, I was shaking from anger and fear, outrage - I was violated! He said nothing, just held me. His quiet strength flowed into my body and I calmed down. There were no words. He just held me and loved me. I was so grateful.*

Over the years I've given that incident much thought. I think the young kid with the box knife was on drugs. His eyes weren't focused at the time, he sort of stared off into the darkness.

When I ripped his jacket, the material was a rag; it was like ripping a piece of tissue paper. After my mind had calmed down and I could see clearly, it was not a Black-White thing; the boy was a lost soul. He needed to be put somewhere that he could be looked after and helped.

My heart went out to him. Apparently there were no Christians in his 'hood to guide him to a better life. The officer who held me during the ride filled me with his understanding of my fear. In his way he was sending a message of we're not "Black" or White; all of us are wounded in some way by ancient hatreds and ignorance.

To this day I am grateful to him for being there, showing kindness and unconditional Love.

What are Christians doing about "helping" the "downtrodden," "poor people" of Chicago, Detroit, Oakland, Memphis, Birmingham, Atlanta, Baltimore... *Americans*... The list goes on. Don't they need saving? Don't they need an education? Of course there's not much glamor in telling your friends, "I was a missionary in Split Lip, Arkansas..." They don't wear colored shawls in Arkansas - they wear bib overalls.

Inner city people don't need wells dug, schools raised or more cattle. They need to be rescued from the drug dealers, the pimps, abusive parents, fast foods - (that is if they're lucky enough to get *any* food), ignorance, self-loathing, welfare humiliation...

The longer people exist in this degradation, the more their souls are damaged, irreparable, the harder the task for Enlightenment is.

Telling friends how you survived a winter saving souls in Tibet, drinking yak milk, repelling a wounded shepherd down a 200

43

foot cliff of sheer ice, is much more captivating than telling how you helped a class of 6 year olds in Canton, OH, learn their colors and make cards for their mothers.

## GANGS - SURROGATE FAMILIES

Again, attending to the high incidence, in America, of single mothers with multiple children, is this an effect of the high rate of crime, the high rate of fatherless children and the low rate of education?

What about children born in these stats who are unsupervised, running around the neighborhoods day and night, no one to worry about them, go look for them - no care at all...no dinner, no baths, no goodnight bedtime kiss...

What about the thousands of foster children, dumped by the mothers, unclaimed by fathers, not wanted by society, who are crime-in-the-wings waiting to come on-stage? Anything for survival.

Thousands of girls running away from home because of parental abuse...? Boys, who have no father, no one to set a good example of manhood - self respect, what about them?

What abut the high rate of gangs in the inner city...? Boys, searching for love and acceptance - a home. Girls searching for love and acceptance - a home. They group together to form "families," but have no concept of how families work. Many gangs turn to crime, hate crimes, violence, to have something to do - to have an identity - a family.

Violence and hatred are their daily companions, their daily diet, their neighborhood schools.

Where are the "Christians?" Are these "countries" - Illinois, Maryland, Alabama - on their lists of places to "save?" Or are these places too dangerous and "hard to reach" - lost?

What about "love?" In what way are we Christians *doing, demonstrating Love*?

"We shall overcome, ..." overcome what? The many times I have heard groups chanting that song, they have never articulated "what..."

Ignorance? Inner city crime? The incessant, gratuitous violence on TV? Not only are we not overcoming it, we watch it - "Friends," nothing but filth; "Frazier," in and out of bed with anyone you meet somewhere...and we cheer them on.

The jails are over-full in most cities. Much of the population is young men.

Why?

These young men, and the young girls, have never had a home, a family, meals on a regular basis, rarely get to school, either too scared to leave the house or there's no one at home to look after them to get them up, dressed and fed.

Are the people in cities really that bad?

I just read F. Luntz book, "What Americas Really want...Really", and he says what Americans really want is..."freedom from fear".

Freedom from fear?

What fear?

Maybe it's what we're just talking about - the gangs, the violence in the city streets, the violence from the "disadvantaged" who

45

seek equal opportunity the fast, easy way - just take what they want.

## IS EDUCATION CRUEL AND UNUSUAL?

Who's going to stop them? The bleeding heart Liberals? Are we feeling sorry for the underprivileged instead of a boring education?

> *I have a friend, a woman, who works for a message delivery service. That company is located in San Francisco and, she told me, every time she has a delivery in Oakland, when she's actually in Oakland, she runs all the red lights and stop signs to get the parcel delivered and then out of town as fast as she can.*

If Oakland is that dangerous, where are the missionaries? Where are the Christians saving the souls of the pimps, drug sellers, the iPhone snatchers, the purse snatchers, the bullies who beat school kids, the juveniles, the downtrodden, underprivileged population in that once beautiful city?

Why aren't the Christians teaching respect, healthy self-respect? proper diet, refusing drugs, dropping out...?

Whey aren't Christians teaching the "natives" how to speak clearly, so the disadvantaged can better express their rights and use them to best advantage? Why aren't the Christians explaining those rights and the limitations of them? No one has carte blanche in society, we all have responsibilities to our neighbors as well as ourselves.

> *My daughter attends a church where the congregation is mainly Mexicans. They speak only Spanish, the priest is from Columbia so he easily communicates with the people. Since this is America and the Mexicans are*

*limited in their ability to communicate easily with potential employers, I offered to teach English at the church after service.*

*My profession is as a college instructor in Communication, I am qualified to teach. And I speak enough Spanish to communicate easily. The priest refused my offer. No reason. What does this tell you?*

Might, force, does not make their rights. Intelligence and education do. In the inner city there is no lack of intelligence, just guidance on the best way to use it.

Why aren't the Christians explaining cause and effect. Explain the need for mainstream language use and comprehension to facilitate success. Explain how lack of social graces impede general acceptance in mainstream society. Strengthen reading comprehension. In most inner city homes there are no books because few people there read and understand the concepts as well as the verbiage.

If you want to be respected in mainstream America, then you have to play the game their way. The "game" is based on the Ten Commandments - but many of the players are motivated by deceit and indifference some of the time. We have to teach right from wrong, teach ethics.

## SKINHEADS

Racists, White Supremacists, Nazi's, Neo Nazi's, Incels, haters - most of these violent, destructive groups are the result of children being born, unwanted, unloved, uncared for; no place in a home or no home at all.

Violence, destruction, anger, hate - what can we expect from children who are raised to hate, even hate themselves. They are taught to recognize they have no value, understand no one cares for them.

Since nothing is sacred to them - not even themselves, they lash out and destroy what is sacred to others. They physically harm others to the point of destroying the soul, the Light of Life; they kill the extensions of family, they cut the ties that hold love together, either by physically killing someone or killing them with drugs.

They are destroying all that represents love in others - they have none, so why should you? Abandoned, loveless, they have nothing to lose.

Their anger is tactile, strong, concrete - they're lashing out, crushing what society feels is good, is wanted, has value. These discarded, ignored young people are "screaming" for attention; violence and hatred are attention-getters. Attention on any level is "love".

And the sad part of this is, we make fun of them. These are needy, lonely, lost souls, and we excuse them - we say "They need help," and walk away.

> *I was at a seedy flea market, outdoors, and was staring at a large poster of two men on motorcycles. They were dressed in leather,metal, chains, had cropped hair, tattoos - in general scared me.*

> *As I was standing, staring at the men in the poster, one of them shown in the photo happened to walk up with a friend and stood in front of the poster - near me.*

> *I froze in fear.*

> *One guy smiled and said, "Hey, look Pete - it's a picture of you!"*

*Pete smiled and put his head down - he was shy! He was so sweet! want to run over and hug him!*

*I didn't.*

*Maybe I should have.*

# IDENTITY

It's human nature to bond, to seek companionship, to want to touch others, feel loved and needed. Children born in a society where they're not wanted, have no place to rest their head - no home, no support have to create a home and family.

They'll attach themselves to the first strong characters that enter their lives.

Motorcycle groups, drug-using groups, hippies, Goths, homeless and "gangs" of kids, The Westside gang, the Pirates, all "families" who believe in themselves and stick close together.

They designate a section of the 'hood as their territory, their "home" - their turf.

> *In college, in a psych class we were assigned a child from Detention. These were all abandoned children.*
>
> *Our task was to befriend them, have fun, go to lunch, etc.*
>
> *My charge was an 11 year old girl. When I picked her up and started to drive off, startled, she said, "Are you gonna leave your turf?!"*
>
> *I said, "I don't have a turf - I go anywhere I want to." She sat, silent, waiting for the sky to fall.*

If she left her turf she would lose her identity, her quasi family - who would she be? Gangs are families bonded out of fear, a need for human touch, a need for assurance of value. Without proper influence and guidance, gangs can easily get self-destructive, be on the wrong side of the law.

## THE POINT THE PRIVILEGED DON'T GET

The word, "privileged" means those people who are better than other people. And, how can you be better than someone unless that "someone" not as good as you are? So, much of the trick of being "better" is to ensure there are people who are "worse."

By keeping selected people locked in inner-city living conditions, keeping them from easy access to better education, denying them easy access to voting, to competent legal access, to medical care, birth control, self respect, jobs, the "privileged" then, remain the status quo.

But, does this contrived, enforced life style makes us better people?

The "underprivileged" people see the chasm between "haves" and "have nots" - the gap between "privileged" and "non privileged."

But rather than challenge the situation on a level playing field, the under-privileged mistakenly assume that physical force will level the playing field and eliminate the opposition - by force, the underprivileged believe then they will emerge victorious.

So wrong.

"Winning" by force, isn't "winning" at all. You gain *bodies*, but not "minds". It's the "mind" that's the challenge. Getting someone to believe in you and follow you, that's the challenge.

Force is conquered by force and defeated by force. It never ends. Force is the easiest and stupidest manner to win, to achieve respect. But, you don't "win" respect - in your conscience - you know you cheated.

And, winning at all odds is not "winning," it's cheating. You can't fool yourself.

*Once in one of my classes we were talking about baseball athletes winning the game through the use of steroids.*

*One student replied that "winning at all costs is the name of the game."*

*"Ok," I said. "Then why not make a robot that instantly knows the angle, distance, height, velocity and composition of the ball and so hits a home run every time...where is the 'game'?"*

*He had no response.*

The way you win a game is by playing by the rules, making yourself equal to, or better than, the opposition. You learn the strategies, the methods, and the thinking of the opposition, then use these techniques to a better advantage than they do, and win.

There is a way both the privileged and the "disenfranchised" population of the inner city can win, and the privileged can remain untouched.

Christians can send teachers, guides, trainers, surrogate mothers and listeners into the inner cities (missionaries) to uplift the disenfranchised, the disadvantaged, the underprivileged into the Light, into the world of cooperation, helping and sharing, a world of enlightenment where force is not necessary and intelligence is common place.

Mozambique, Kenya and The Congo can manage with lesser help for a short time while we lift America out of the swamp of high crime statistics.

# ABORTION

"Don't worry about abortion, forget It - just like you do the thousands of foster kids."

Let's all agree, abortion is wrong.

But, a great many pregnancies are not wanted, not prepared for, cannot afford, was caused by trauma, the girl is a "special needs" - helpless ... we cannot have a blanket no-abortion stance.

Those people who refuse to consider special circumstances in abortion needs, should sign a statement saying "I will take all responsibility for the care of xxxxxxx's unborn child. She was impregnated under events for which she had no control. She does not want the child, so I will assume all responsibility for the child until it's 21." Then sign this with witnesses.

*There was a court case, I believe in Chicago, where a thirteen year old girl petitioned the court for an abortion. The judge denied her request. She'd been impregnated by her uncle.*

*One year later the same girl appeared before the same judge and sentenced to one year in prison for being an unfit mother.*

A 14 year old child - an unfit mother! She should be outside, in the fresh air, playing ball, walking to the 7-11 for an ice cream - her life was stolen from her!

Where are the Right to Life people, the Pro Life people with their banners denying abortion rights for victims of incest and rape?

If they really cared about Life, then they would adopt unwanted children, foster children, homeless children - but these Christians won't adopt because they're phonies - they speak out of both sides of their mouth.

Are these people doing the work of Jesus? You can lie to yourself. but you can't lie to Him.

*"I do not believe that just because you're opposed to abortion, that that makes you pro-life. In fact I think in many cases, your morality is deeply lacking if at all you want is a child born but not a child fed, not a child educated, not a child housed. And why would I think that you don't? Because you don't want any tax money to go there.*

*That's not pro-life. That's pro birth. We need a much broader conversation on what the morality of pro-life is." Sister Joan Chittister OSB 2019*

The words, "pro birth, not "pro" life are critical in understanding what someone is really saying. "Pro" life is exactly that - a *life*-time commitment to the welfare of that child - commitment for LIFE. A home, education, healthy meals, clean clothes, dental care, immunization shots, piano lessons, braces, helping with homework - this is pro-life.

"Pro" birth means giving birth to a child and then setting it down on a table marked, "FREE" - help yourself."

Which one are *you* doing?

# ALABAMA SIGNS NEAR-TOTAL ABORTION LAW

Kay Ivey, Governor of Alabama, has made it almost impossible for anyone to get an abortion. Most of the people of Alabama agree this is a good thing.

And, to ease this problem, does Alabama provide sex education, birth control information, child rearing guidance, help, for unmarried, abandoned mothers?

No. They have almost outlawed abortion. Well, that figures. Out of the 600,000+ population on welfare, 13% are children on welfare.

Alabama ranks 49 out of 50 for the state education level. So, at that educational level, you can see why they voted for Kay.

With little education and birth control questionable, Alabamans walk with the dinosaurs. And, they're proud of it.

I suggest this law is evil - it's punitive. It's a way to punish women and keep them under "control." It's Old Testament thinking, punishment oriented. Usually married women have no need for abortion. They have a steady income, a husband to help with the care and guidance of the children.

So therefore the law seems limited to grievously restricting the possible needs of unmarried girls, wives abandoned by husbands, children impregnated by their uncles, impregnated by incest, impregnated by rape…

Apparently Kay is out of child-rearing age, so she doesn't fear the consequences of rape. Possibly in her case, as the French say, "If you can't stop it, just lay back and enjoy it."

Why do some Christians deny the existence of the pain, the humiliation and trauma from rape in women? Why do people of little education and no human warmth deny children and abused women the right to a good life? What would Jesus say?

# ADAM AND PREGNANCY

Because Adam bit the apple - of *his own free will*, and then God forced both Adam and Eve out of Paradise, women are held accountable for their Fall from Grace.

That conclusion is vacuous.

If we believe that abortion is against the will of God, then it's up to us Christians, to give better guidance to young girls, **before** they get pregnant. Tell them the truth about sex - it's NOT love, it's SEX.

With some men, when the sex is over, the girl is over, "love" is over.

It may seem that there's not much concern for the boys in both abortion issues and in birth control issues. They don't get involved - after the fact.

It's up to us Christians to stop the tidal wave of unwanted children, the ones that run wild on the city streets, the ones that sleep in alley ways, on park benches. The ones that seek comfort and love by belonging to a gang. The children who turn to violence as revenge for not being wanted, not loved this who see Life as a place of fear that needs to be controlled, dominated by force.

But, occasionally the sun splashes through the darkness of homeless, abandoned souls and brings the Light of Hope.

*I was in Manila for a few days. Since the sun is bright very early, I left my hotel at 6:00 a.m. for a brief walk around that beautiful city.*

*I passed by a shop where several boys were piled in a heap, sound asleep. The boys were around 6 - 9 years in age.*

*One boy extricated himself from the pile, came up to me and said, "Lady, you give me a nickel!"*

*I looked down into that adorable face and asked, "Why should I give you a nickel?"*

*"Because I'm hungry. I want breakfast."*

*There was a small cafe open close by.*

*I said, "Ok," and we went in the cafe. I told the boy, "Get anything you want."*

*A huge chocolate cake was on display. I assumed he'd want some and I was ok with that. Also a long bunch of bananas lie across the top of the counter.*

*He pointed up at the bananas. "I want that!"*

*"You want a banana?"*

*"No! I want that!" He wanted the stalk of bananas! Maybe about 15 on the stalk.*

*The clerk said, "Who's gonna pay for this, lady?" (5 cents a banana!)*

*"I am." and we walked out, the stalk firmly in his grip.*

*Suddenly the tangle of boys unwound and each boy grabbed a piece of fruit and dug in.*

*My young host waited 'til everyone was eating and then he took his fruit to eat last.*

I stood, spellbound! I was moved by his grace, his willingness to share, the sense of satisfaction in himself and his "family." It was Love, pure, open unqualified, Love.

Who were these children, where are they from? I wish I could bring them all home with me - they could have bananas every day!

## CHILD ABUSE

As adults, no, they won't "get over it…," no they won't "forget it." It lives on each day of their life. And when you complain about fear, hatred or anger about the abuse, the standard lines are:

get on with your life

you have to forgive

think of something else

just put it out of your mind

maybe you misunderstood

it wasn't that bad

it's not like that

it was only once

it was a mistake

Smile, Jesus loves you

You take things too seriously

When you're a child raised in the "inner city," abuse is a common, daily, occurrence. When people are frustrated, limited in their choices, have little understanding of what Life expects of them, they lash out and children are the easiest targets on which to release frustration. They can't fight back. And usually, they're afraid to tell anyone - who cares?

But, for sure, *they don't forget.*

Then, these unwanted, unloved, abused children abuse animals, each other and become fodder for the penal system, jail is a revolving door. Who is there to help them, to teach them, show them a better choice of life?

Christian missionaries?

## PREGNANCY, OUTSIDE OF MARRIAGE AS PUNISHMENT

It's all her fault. There is one religion that actually states that if a girl gets pregnant, it's "*her* mistake."

HER mistake!! All hers, all alone, she did it - SHE made a mistake! As a Communication Studies Instructor, I see a deep hatred of women in that belief. The female has been singled out as the "sinner," only she sinned. What a strong statement of HATE - and we do it to ourselves! We teach hate! Christians teach hate!

Let's look at the "truth" about the "mistake."

A girl *cannot* get pregnant! **A GIRL** <u>CAN NOT</u> **GET PREGNANT.**

A girl is an empty vessel, a bowl, a pot - she cannot impregnate herself. She needs an outside agent to *impregnate her.*

She does not get pregnant alone! Pregnancy is not **HER** mistake!

And yet, society, religions, friends, neighbors, family - her church, hold her responsible! This is beyond stupidity, cruel and heartless. Religions blame women in general on Eve for the reason for the Fall of paradise.

Yes, Eve, a young woman who had no training, no upbringing, no sense of right or wrong. God told her **AND** Adam not to eat the fruit of a certain tree. But He didn't say anything about serpents, guile and subterfuge. Eve had no concept of lies, deceit… she was innocent.

So the serpent conned her into taking a bite of the fruit of wisdom and it was pretty good. So, Eve called to Adam, "Hey, ya wanna bite?" Adam said, "Ok." and took a chunk out of the fruit of knowledge.

Then God comes along and asks, "Who bit this fruit?" - knowing full well what had happened.

Adam, immediately jumped up and said, 'SHE made me do it! It's not my fault!"

So God kicked them both out of Paradise, Eve for disobeying Him, and Adam for being a jerk. I've often wondered how Eve could force Adam to take a bite of fruit when she was only the size of a rib…? 20"…?

*In a doctor's office I happened to read a copy of the Watchtower magazine. In it was an article about Adam - not Eve. I read the article, it was vacuous and concluded that Adam was a wonderful man.*

*Wonderful? What did he do that was even remotely "wonderful"? I'll be wondering about that for Eternity.*

Women, girls, are trained one way and boys, men are trained another.

A young girl thinks "I'm 'in love', and he loves me." She'll have sex just this once - I mean it would make *him* happy!...

you can't get pregnant the first time..."

She's ecstatic to think that she'll make *him* happy by giving herself over to him.

And the young boy thinks, "WOW! I scored!"

With males, sex is clinical, with girls it's emotional.

Girls are taught by the media that sex and love are the same thing.

The media also suggests that if you use the right toothpaste, you'll marry a rich guy.

Girls are trained to make themselves desirable, attractive to men. There are literally thousands of ads, on TV, magazines, sales signs, and other women, demanding that girls, lose weight, gain weight, get longer lashes, longer hair, better complexion, lighter skin, darker skin, bigger breasts, bigger hips, shorter skirts, briefer material in her clothes - it never ends.

Girls don't understand that when it's acceptable in society to wear brief clothing, and when a man sees you, he can't tell the difference between an innocent young girl, a well dressed young lady and one who might be "available."

They all look the same to him.

There are men who will accost any girl to satisfy their needs of the moment. This is why it's so critical to dress as though a girl has pride in herself and her body.

*On one news program a girl was suing some man for taking photos of her*

> *under her skirt. I wondered,*
> *"Where was he when he took the photos…across the street?"*

We set men up to "tease" them and then punish them for doing what they think they have the freedom, the social sanction - the training, to do. And then, when the men think we're lusting after them, we trick them. We send out a message, "Hi, big guy…come and get me…" and when they do…we get mad. They get confused.

Women should ask men, "What thoughts go through your mind when you see young girls with short dresses that partly display their gender?" Both the low tops of the dresses and the high tops of the skirt send a very clear message to some men.

Perhaps it's time to reverse the styles - top up, bottom down. This way maybe the girls will send the idea of self respect - girls will always be beautiful anyway.

# THE MEDIA

In my Communication classes I have advised the students not to believe *anything* on the media.

## TERMINOLOGY

In my classes I never allowed any vulgar, scatological words. Those words are superfluous and bring the level of communication down to a point where intelligence is meaningless.

And, yet, much of the time on TV and in daily life, the "F…" word is every other word. The meaning of the word reflects on the speaker, a person of low education, insults the listener, has no intelligent argument, and is seeking attention to offset self-perception of low esteem. Saying the "F" word in causal conversation is a way to establish one's self as urbane, sophisticated. It's free speech.

It is pathetic.

*My students were walking into the classroom to take the Midterm test. I like them to be calm and relaxed during tests so they'll do well.*

*A student from the previous class was sitting there working on his computer.*

*I said, "I'm sorry, but you'll have to leave. This room is for my students to take their Midterm.*

*Without looking up, he said, "F…* **\* YOU!** *WHAT?*

*I was stunned!*

*I told him again to leave. Again, he said, "**F...\* YOU!**"*

*I took him to Student Court where two male students judged him. I wanted him expelled. His behavior was egregious, insulting to anyone, but especially to an Instructor! After hearing his side and my side, the two "judges" said, "Your punishment is that you cannot go to any parties this quarter."!*

*The boys smiled at each other and left. I felt like I'd been slapped in the face!*

*These are the people we are raising today, drug pushers, rapers, politicians, the Brett Kavanaugh's who make a laughing stock out of innocence, courtesy and decency.*

Is this who we're raising in America, the sanctuary of Christians? I was so-o disgusted with the behavior and message of these young men. Think of the examples of behavior these young men set for children - pretty offal.

And, we're going downhill from there.

A Christian and a person of self respect has far more sophisticated means of communication - intelligent words, expressed in a clear, coherent manner.

And yet, we, the public, have the power to stop this unwelcome style of speech simply by saying, "Stop it." Yes, it's a land of free speech, I have mentioned that before. So we are free to say, "Stop it!" We can refuse to respond to any language that is not appreciated in our world.

But, free speech goes in two directions. Anyone can say what words they want and I can walk away, tell the media that I am offended, take it off the air, I won't buy your products… free speech is a useful weapon with sharp blades.

Free speech is used to bully people; un-named, faceless specters that weak willed, young and inexperienced people take seriously. Some people, in particular teenagers, have little self esteem; they don't yet know their value and strengths.

So they absorb the negativity and criticism and become depressed. From there it's easy to segue into drugs and worse - suicide.

## TAKE A PILL

Yes, take a pill. Tired, depressed, too fat, too thin, too weak, going bald, thin hair, legs hurt, back hurts, need energy, nervous energy, can't sleep?

What ever it is, take a pill, take two - take 3. If one is good, three is better.

And then we wonder why our kids take pills, all colors, all kinds from the medicine cabinet, share at school, steal, an endless stream of pills for everything and if those don't cover it, more on the way.

And then we wonder what happened? KayLee never took drugs before and now she's in Emergency. RJ was at a frat party and they thought he was asleep, but they couldn't revive him.

Pills, hypochondria, self absorption, experiments, advice of friends - American society is a sick society and pills won't fix it.

Have a salad, fresh fruit, fresh vegetables, drink cold water from the tap. Don't have dessert… they're a chemical waste land. Stick with fruit.

Shut off the TV, read, talk, play Monopoly, play the piano. Can't sleep? Run around the block twice, shower and fall asleep, happily, in bed.

The stress of making money, keeping up with whatever istuff is new, how can we afford… braces, donations… we are under incredible stress then, take a pill. The media says it's what I need.

No, you don't. You are being manipulated for the bottom line; you're being used, manipulated and made a fool of.

Many times I have mentioned a specific religion where women are strongly controlled. I have noticed there is a high rate of migraine headaches in these women - wives, specifically. It seems there may be a *cause* for migraines that a pill can't fix. So, instead of eliminating the *cause* of the migraine, women are encouraged to deaden the pain by artificial means and kill their soul.

# THERAPISTS, PSYCHOLOGISTS, GURUS, SURI

At this stage of history technology as usurped humanity. We turn to little red lights and brightly colored sliding circles on hand-held devices for comfort and solace.

We can consult oracles, "Suri, where can I get ming pow chow in my neighborhood?" And Suri replies, "You had that last night. Get a 4 layer burger tonight, 2 for $5.00 at the gas station."

There are therapists on call, your own psychologist who asks you,"How do you feel about that?" That's not a solution to loneliness or despair.

We should turn to the New Testament for guidance - it's all there. Listen to the Prince of Peace and "he will give you rest."

## SUICIDE

From drugs, low self-esteem, exchange of unacceptable personal information and unacceptable photo exchange, we segue into meeting *anyone* on the media. Nameless faces, nameless voices who influence our children to do, to say and reveal secrets that should be shared only with family.

The weak, young minds of our children are encouraged to "just try this, smoke this, shoot this, inhale this…it's not habit-forming…" and then after they're addicted, we parents step in and sweep up the pieces.

*Just a few moments ago on our neighborhood link, one man asked if he should take a certain pill for pain, did anyone know if it were addictive?*

*His doctor had prescribed it. I said, "No, don't take it. Take a shower, take a nap. Don't start on pills."*

*Another neighbor said, "Go ahead take them. They're not addictive - I take them; if I don't I can't sleep."*

*"…not addictive, but, if I don't take 'em I 'can't sleep.'"*

You see what I mean? How easy it is to get hooked?

Once, to get me to lose weight, a friend slipped some pills in my pocket, "Here, take these."

When she left, I threw them out.

When our teens and younger children are investing their trust in sadistic, warped guidance over the media and they're prodded into suicide, we're surprised.

From what I have read the teens are depressed, feel isolated, unloved, not attractive, don't measure up to expectations. Why? They have every THING they want.

Are they loved? Assured of their worth? Is the family cohesive, caring for each other…or is love tentative…?

As of today children as young as 5 years old up to teens are encouraged, guided and praised for committing suicide.

## *This is evil - pure, evil.*

Where are the parents? Why do we allow this? What are we doing so stupidly that we allow these evil forces to lead our children to drugs, and the most evil act possible…

> *suicide.*

That is the most heinous act against the Will of God.

## TREND SETTERS

The media, the "games," internet, social media and ads are all gauged to subvert young minds for profit or fame. The rock "stars", male and female, for the most part are characters of humans. They display hair do's of any imaginable style and lips are colored in what gets attention. Art is not an issue - attention is. Blank, ghoulish eyes colored to appear as vampires and with the piercings and tattoos create a walking circus.

Breasts on rock stars are pumped up so high they can double as hot-air balloons. Hip muscles, the rear end, are pumped up so big they can act as a day bed for a passerby.

The result is, our children watch these clowns and understand this is ok, the stars can do it, so can I.

Christians, are these healthy models for our youngsters to follow? We can change it all by a phone call, a letter, email or march with banners.

The media, that we all support, has created a population of girls for sale. The program, "The Bachelorette" does everything but put the girls up on an auction block. The program humiliates girls, but, like Eve, they're not trained to understand how cheap they look, how cheap. silly, immature they act - it's all about making $ for the advertisers.

*In my Communication classes, I call attention to the tasteless mode of ripped jeans, embarrassingly short skirts, blouses open down to their bottom rib.*

*Then in contrast, I showed photos of women, beautifully dressed, hair neatly done, minimal makeup, minimal jewelry and no holes in their nose or tattoos.*

*I showed the girls how beautiful they are just as they are. Young, happy and healthy are the best beauty aids there are.*

*I want them to communicate self-pride, self respect in the way they dress.*

In a way, I can understand the dress requirements of most Muslim women. They often are required to be covered from head to toe, and in extreme cases, even the eyes are covered by a black veil.

This way men cannot "lust" over their hair or their ankles. The women are covered to save men from lusting after them.

The women my be repressed by Western standards, but they're not fools.

# SEX EDUCATION:

## Girls can be attractive and proud of themselves, not a help-yourself buffet for males.

What girls need to understand is, it's not "love" that attracts men to you - most boys are a bulging bag of churning sex drive - they want sex, SEX, and lots of it - with anyone!

Any time! Any place!

There is no way sex can be controlled. It has no "off" switch. It's the same now as it was in the beginning - and ever shall be.

In some religions, sex outside of marriage is a sin.

Are you kidding?

Then there are more sinners than can fit in heaven, and God put sex there for a purpose.

Many churches and other organizations focus on physical activities for boys - get their mind and energy going in a productive direction. In general, boys are inquisitive, curious, creative, problem-solvers, high energy beings, they like each other - and, usually, they are very likable.

We need to do the same for girls. And, I'm suggesting that physical activities are great and also, perhaps for girls, we could focus on their problem-solving acumen. Teach them to think, to analyze situations, cause and effect, learn to reason, sharpen relationship skills and master basic physics to stimulate their intelligence and independence in decision-making.

# THE ANTICHRIST:

## The enemy within

Christians, do any of you know what the "anti" christ is? Do you know what the word means?

"Anti" means "against", to be passionately, firmly and perhaps, irrationally, opposed to something.

As far as I know, the word, "Christ," is a title of great reverence and esteem.

The title, "Christ", is ancient and is a sort of "blessing" for extraordinary achievement in the spiritual domain. The "Christ's" over the centuries have been very few, *very few,* and we Christians are so blessed as to have Jesus, whom we believe to be **the** Christ, sent as an emissary, teacher and protector to guide us to the right way to

Live and work with each other.

Already in our midst, the Anti Christ has insinuated itself into the fiber of our thinking and acting, little by little. We tolerate the slow, creeping Evil of the Anti Christ because we don't believe it has that much power. We are taught to tolerate difference; if a religion is different than Christianity, we allow for its existence - we give it room and sanction its beliefs and observances.

Buddhists have no God as Christians do. But they are not "against" Christians. They live, meditate, behave in a quiet, unintrusive way so as not to disturb other worshippers. Their good thoughts are a blessing to the world.

They would never try to change us, usurp us, condemn us. Their thoughts and actions are to lift up the world. They are vegetarians usually, no alcohol, no drugs, no slander... they are people of peace.

Christians could learn a lot from them.

But, the "anti" Christ is against everything Christians believe in, the freedom to worship God in our own way. We have invited an asp into our bosom and it is anxious to bite us and destroy us.

The Anti Christ is not bogged down with ethics, fairness, sharing - it is a force created to destroy all thought, all education, any semblance of free will. And we Christians clutch this evil in a warm embrace.

In particular, in the inner city, the Anti Christ has established fertile roots. Evil takes root in ignorance and poverty. Evil, like the serpent in the tree - a serpent insinuating revolution in the minds of depressed people, uses arguments, examples, and lies to get a foothold toward the destruction of Christianity.

And we Christians allow it, ignore it, sanction it.

The Anti Christ is gaining ground in the inner city, especially in the prisons. We Christians are looking the other way thinking we're practicing diversity, acceptance of difference.

A Christian's mission is to venture into the depths of the big cities and bring the Light, the Truth and the Way into the darkest corners, the alley ways, the stairwells,

the trashed empty houses.

Christians must put on the whole armor of God.

## LOVE THE SINNER

Christians are taught there is only one way to live, and that is the way our Savior taught us, LOVE ye one another, as he loves us.

Now, is this "love" carte blanche? - does it include *everyone*? The Bible warns us of an "anti" Christ, an antichrist is here to destroy Christians - that is in the present tense, *an Anti Christ is here to destroy us.*

Should we love that which seeks to destroy the very thing Christ came to teach us?

Is it possible we can "love" something even as we're told to destroy it?

Diseases…do we "hate" cancer, or is it a dis-ease which much be checked, eliminated? Do we "hate" dementia, or is it a dis-ease that destroys life? Is it possible we can understand the evil - the dis-ease, of the antichrist is not necessarily something to "hate," but rather be cured…? Eliminated…?

And "sin", is it a matter of social preference, cultural teaching? We have the 10 Commandments and yet we support TV and media which explains that to be socially acceptable, voted for, popular, we need to behave in a manner that goes against God's teachings - and we gladly do it - and, excuse it, "Well, whaddya gonna do - everybody has one, is doing it, says it's ok, don't be so serious, just put it in God's hands…"

## THE TROJAN WAR

Mythology tells the story of a war between the Greeks and the Trojans. The myth goes that among the prominent cultures were the Greeks and the Trojans. Both cultures were war-like, had armies, Generals, sub-ordinates - all the latest equipment and incentive needed to kill each other, or anyone else, but especially each other.

You know how it is, sometimes you meet someone you just don't like? No reason, well… maybe they're taller, better looking, richer, stronger, have a faster chariot than you do… that sort of thing. So, you want them eliminated - and fast!

The Greeks were excellent at games, marathons, discus throwing, javelins, pondering the universe and peeling grapes. They had the latest iphones, togas from third world countries at exorbitant prices, self-driving chariots - they were warriors of some distinction, fearless and well-trained. Their prowess at battle was legendary. Their record at battle was as winners - they always won.

They were very proud of themselves and had a lot of banquets where they applauded themselves and had virgin servers - in diaphanous gowns.

One afternoon the Greeks decided to conquerer the Trojans - it took 10 years of siege and the Trojans held fast. The Trojans would never admit to defeat, they were complacent in their past and watched TV shows that enforced their belief of greatness. So what to do?

On the out side of the city walls, the Greeks decided they would sail away, which was an indication of defeat. But, before they left, they built a handsome gift for the Trojans as a sort of apology for the 10 year inconvenience.

The Greeks built a handsome, huge horse, and, as an added touch of irony, enclosed a group of soldiers who were a sort of a surprise gift for the Trojans.

Sure enough, the Trojans believed that the Greeks were good guys, just "misunderstood -you can't judge people; we're all good. The Trojans graciously accepted the gift, hauled it into the city, then at night the Greek soldiers descended from inside the horse and killed everyone.

This is similar to the Anti Christ. Do you really think that anyone seeking to destroy Christianity will do so in the open? Do you really think they'll come out in the open with their sabres drawn, ululating their battle cry?

Or will they smirk at Americans by stating that it is their right in America to remove all symbols, all traces of Christianity from the basic structure of American life - the very reason we came to this country - to worship God in the Christian way?

They point out that we have "separation of church from state."

However, this same force has managed to get serving pork removed from some school cafeterias and has managed to stop us from saluting the flag in classrooms.

They stand together, enforce their laws, but deny us ours - and, we let them!

Because, like the Trojans, we Americans tend to pat ourselves on the back and say, "I'm great - no one can fool me! That big horse is a sign of capitulation."

"Pride goeth before a fall"

## AMERICA - *UNDER GOD*

If you're familiar with history of the early times in Europe, in the 1500's, or so, in Western history, you were either a Catholic or you died in unpleasant ways. Sometimes you were tortured to death, sometimes burned alive, so then you'd understand the desperate need to escape to a country where you could worship God in your own way, unmolested.

People, under great peril to themselves and families, escaped smothering religious oppression to find a new country where they could live in peace, to worship God in comfort.

And, so against all odds, Christians came to the New World.

But, here again, Americans were greatly restrained by Old World laws and traditions. We weren't "free" - it was not "our" country - yet. We were forced to obey a "king," a ruler that still attempted to keep us under control in all walks of life.

America, under God, rebelled and, again in great danger, we came close to losing our hard-won freedom. God sent us the strength and wisdom to overcome the enemy.

Now we have another enemy in our midst, and, under our Constitution, they have a right to be here. But, like the Trojan horse, we have invited in a religion diametrically opposed to ours, and one that will never relinquish a passion to destroy the Christian way of life.

This is why we need missionaries in the neighborhoods of the "disadvantaged, downtrodden, under-privileged..." population.

The serpent slides down from the tree and teaches the people how "his religion will take them out of this poverty, take them to a place where everybody has everything, kill a Christian and gain a place in Heaven, get even with Capitalism for keeping you oppressed..."

The serpent is offering the lost, lonely, desperate people a free ride on the yellow brick road to Paradise.

And of course, people who have nothing, who are lost, who have no hope, no love, no future except Suicide by Cop, listen and believe what they hear. They have nothing to lose.

There are songs written to the glory of "Suicide by Cop." The lyrics will break your heart, they boil with emptiness, aloneness, sorrow, grief... so sad...

The Anti Christ has fertile ground to plant seeds - and America is providing free water. We want to be fair...

Christians believe in diversity, everyone is good if given a chance.

Was Charles Manson basically good? Hitler? Jack the Ripper?

"Wake for the night is coming..." Time is running out.

# AMERICAN GOVERNMENT

It's 2019. At this point, with Twitter, ABC, NBC, streaming news, Cloud, we can get the latest "information" about our government each moment. Bickering, he did this - he did that, she said, he said, they said - it's sickening!

So many of our elected officials, men and women chosen from the best the nation has to offer are behaving like kindergarteners. Our leader is an international humiliation - a buffoon. We voted for him.

The person we voted against was, in my observation, mad, insane, irrational.

Is this all we have to offer in this country, the greatest in the world, the highest educated and the healthiest... we like to think.

And those that didn't vote for him held thousands of rallies, protests, smashing store window, smashing windshields of citizens, blocking motor traffic highways... protesting our right to vote for someone they don't like.

And we say there's no Anti Christ? He's hard at work and we're paying him overtime.

It's sick. We're all sick. We are the government and we is sick.

Some years ago I was delighted to be a part of the presidential campaign. I stumped for the candidate, met him a few times and went to his main rally in San Francisco. While there, at the rally, as a cheer leader, I was beaten up by some of the team who didn't like my candidate. I saw another cheer leader knocked down and kicked at the rally by political henchmen. The police and CBS cameraman turned their backs on us and walked away.

I protested the incidents - in my torn clothes and bruises, but people just walked away, especially the police.

I gave up on politics. I am so disgusted. I vote, yes, but I know now that everything you see on the news is a lie.

"Absolute power corrupts absolutely" is a quote from Baron Acton in the 1800's.

He observed, "Power tends to corrupt, and absolute power corrupts absolutely. Great men are almost always bad men."

Oo - that hurts. But true.

Why are they "bad"? Because we let them. We vote them in. We defend them.

We make fun of them. It's entertainment.

And the churning, the swill in government, simply reflects the will of the people. There are no longer Republicans or Democrats. There are "Neo Nazi's", liberals who control your thinking, your rights.

Where are the Christians?

They're in the thick of it. Rather than voting for Christians who uphold the morals of society, instead of insisting on ethics, we pander to the "liberals" who talk about "rights" - the right to swear against God in public, the right to advocate sex as you feel like it, with whom you feel like it, where you feel like it - on TV, for example.

The "games" for kids to learn to slaughter their opponent, to laugh when someone is suffering. The school shootings, the open drug use, the presence of drug pushers at the schools, on the sidewalks,

Do you really think that George Bush, when he went to Alabama, to a Baptist church, and stood in the Baptist choir, surrounded by choir members, under a cross…really cared about where he was?

Uh, no.

And he gave $1,000,000.00 - *one million dollars* to the Southern Baptists to fight abortion! I didn't vote for that..who voted for that? Isn't that taxpayer money? How does anyone have the right to give tax payer money to a specific non-profit organization for its political agenda?

He was buying minority votes. So obvious.

Did he get a receipt?

No.

Was that separation of church and state?

No.

And, we let him. And they took it. Was it kosher…no. Was it clean money…no. Was it his money…no. It was stolen from the coffers of Americans for health care, food programs, building schools…

"Do as I say, not as I do…"

This country is on free fall, rolling down hill in a super-powered SUV with no brakes.

Jack Kennedy and his women-on-call for the moment. Bill Clinton and his affairs splashed across the tabloids.

These are our leaders! These are the men who we hold up as examples of strength and guidance to our children.

And we Americans, Christians, find it amusing; covertly we sanction it.

Rashida Tlaib, just on Google, called the President a "MF," but not just the initials she actually said the words! Several people in the area gave the President the finger. Doesn't Rashida realize the sewage that drops from her lips tells us all who *she really* is…? A verbal porta-potty? And…we ALLOW IT!

This is slanderous to the nation, not acceptable - this has nothing to do with political parties, it has to do with insulting the American people. Are we going to allow ourselves to be so debased?

Christians, where in Hell are you? In the front seat of your SUV, driving to the fiery pit??

# OUT-DATED TERMINOLOGY

Today we have "dumbed down" education to the point where script is not taught, "big" words are avoided - I mean, actually, TDL! DYTS? LLMG!!

We're back to carving petroglyphs, stone-writing done on a ipad.

Words have very little use today - people don't use them, they don't need them. A machine does all our thinking. The media controls our thoughts, our needs and our behavior.

Often Christians approach a possible convert and say, "Jesus died for your sins. Jesus loves you."

What "sins"? What "love"?

*When I was young girl, another young girl walked up to me and said, "I've been washed in the blood of the lamb."*

*I am an animal lover and when she said to me she had killed a lamb and washed in its blood, it made me sick.*

*I was disgusted.*

This is a classic example of why Christian idioms need to change, be up-dated. This is a phrase from Fundamentalists' archaic thinking. Yes, Jesus died for our sins, but can we phrase that so it relates to today's understanding of the power, the unconditional love Jesus has for every person?

# YOUR WORDS - MY WORDS - PRAYER

A encyclopedia of idioms, terminology, concocted phrases and obscure concepts are created to separate the unwashed from the elite in religious organizations. They serve to annoy other denominations, confuse converts and slow down their conversations with Jesus. To pray to Jesus, you need an interpreter of their choice.

That way you won't wander off their path into independent thinking.

I understand some people don't pray because they don't know what words to use. "Hello, God," works fine if that's all you have. I used to say, "Hello, God, it's me again, Carolyn." Then say what I had to say, just talk.

One great thing about God, He's always home. You can knock and then walk right in. He understands why you're there and is always listening.

And again, it helps if you have a little prayer nearby to help you move out of a tight situation, something you can easily memorize and say quickly.

I had a friend who told me angels actually help her with the housework! She'd say, "Angels, please help me lift this chair, I want to vacuum under it."

And, she says, they helped her.

Here's a list of words that may need to be set aside from use in the inner city lingo, they're far too esoteric:

APOSTOLIC

BAPTIST

BEATIFICATION

COMPASSION

CONFRATERNAL

CONSCRATION

ENCOUNTER

EPISCOPAL

EUCHARIST

EVANGELICAL

INDULGENCE

INFALLIBILITY

PROFESS

PENTECOSTAL

REDEMPTION

RESTORATION

SANCTIFY

TRANSFORMATION

VENERATE - and, oh, yes…

PRESBYTERIAN - took me ages to pronounce that. What does it mean?

All these words and more, are created, purposefully as a separate language for a specific denomination as a closed club. They are "lingo," a special, separate vocabulary created for that particular belief system.

This lingo *keeps people out*, rather than invites them in. Lingo is designed to separate one denomination from a more "elite" one - they're meaningless to someone who cannot even wade through the daily, convoluted babble of mainstream society.

Very possibly the "convert" is someone who was not wanted as a child, unexpected, unplanned for and is a problem to feed and provide for. The "convert" has found food in garbage cans, stolen it from 7/11 stores - donuts, chips, candy...

Saying to someone, "Jesus is infallible. Our church is evangelical and we have indulgences to sanctify the transformation of the uninitiated into our confraternal fellowship," is, actually, basically, unequivocally like a sure fire way to scare off people who only, like, use amazing one-syllable words.

Having a warm smile and the empty words, "Jesus loves you..." is meaningless. The soup kitchens speak the loudest. Who can hear the word "love" on an empty stomach? A hot bowl of stew, a warm shower and a bed for the night speak loudly.

No need for words.

Jesus fed thousands with bread and fish. Yes, he gave a long speech too, but He knew words mean nothing unless you can get someone's attention first. He went among the people, all people, not just "needy", underprivileged people. He lived with them, ate with them - he did not feed them empty words.

The woman at the well, the woman being stoned, Martha washing his feet in expensive oil - he sat with them, was with them, cared about them, listened to them, understood them.

He didn't set a donation at their front door and leave.

In my talks at the jail ministry I often comment on the willingness of Jesus to listen to women and respond appropriately to their feelings and needs.

He didn't say, "I've been meaning too, don't have the time, I wish I could do more, I know I should…" - "I went on a march…"

He gave himself. He cares. He listens.

# WOMEN'S LIB et al

## MARRIAGE

Over the centuries women have been lied to, used, abused, *forced* into loveless marriages, *forced* to have children, wanted or not, and, they're told, "It's your duty." All this based on opinion, society's opinion and what's in the Old Testament.

Women are exhorted to marry and breed - in the **Old** Testament. But wait - doesn't it also say,

> "Do not yoke a donkey and an ox together..."?

Intelligence, common sense and human limitations are not usually accounted for in a forced marriage. With most Christian denominations today much lip service is given to women, lots of empty praise, but they're given very little authority and rarely allowed input in executive decisions.

The goal of marriage seems to be to get women locked into a commitment as soon as possible, before they can make mature decisions of that magnitude.

Husbands, fathers often walk out on a marriage or relationship to find a better life for themselves. The one they created and swore to uphold, is too stressful.

Women are left with the grievous responsibility of maintaining the family, raising the children, being a good model, providing the children with a good meal. To provide for the children women have to work, do what work they can get, work alongside men who get almost double the money women make for the same work. It's a problem finding affordable child care and paying for it, then women are censored for not being there for the children.

*They're sick of it.*

So, because women are ignored, censored, abandoned and ridiculed by society, Christians - they snap - they have nothing to lose. They're already "lost" to society.

So, they put the children in a car and push the car into the sea. We drown them in bathtubs. We set the house on fire with the children in their beds, or, the mothers too, leave, never to be seen again.

*I knew this Christian woman who had 5 sons. After years of housework, mothering, diligent attention to the family, she snapped.*

*She told me, Carolyn, I had had it. I couldn't take any more. I walked out of the house, shut the screen door and never looked back.*

I happened to be at her apartment one day when one of her sons came to the door, he had tracked her down.

She talked to him through the screen door and told him to leave, she wanted nothing to do with him. I felt so bad for him. He left. He was a casualty of society's impossible, relentless demands on a woman.

In France, and Sweden, the country provides child care for the first two years of the baby's life to give the mother a chance to recover her energy. The system has flaws, it's run by the government, but the point is, the mothers are given consideration, their lack of energy, physical and mental stress are accounted for.

The ancient teachings of holding women in low esteem are over. We need to concentrate on the NEW Testament - the words of

Jesus. He said that God made males and females, therefore a man shall leave his parents and join his wife as one person.

"What therefore **God** has joined together, let not man separate."
Matt:19

Ambiguous.

What "**God**" has joined together, don't let any person come between them. How do we know when *God* has "joined" someone together? Is it because they're of age? Is it because the church needs new members? Is it because you're getting old and you don't want to be alone? Is it because no one else is available, he's leaving for war, this is your chance to "get a man"?

The answer is, we don't know. We cannot force people into marriage, although most religions do try, in fact, insist on it.

I know of marriages when, after 60, 75 years, the couple is still together and respect each other. That, truly, is a marriage made in heaven.

One religion orders women to get married and breed as many children as possible. The men of that belief system become the One God after they die and get their own solar system.

The question nags me, "How do millions of men become individual *ONE* Gods?"

They choose one woman to populate their planet and she is given the "honor" of incessant breeding for Eternity.

Now, there's an offer you can't refuse! Populate your own planet! I'd like a planet with all red heads, musicians and good cooks, thank you.

88

When a woman breaks down, has excessive emotional stress, she's told, "Take it to the lord in prayer." Then, in the Bible we're told, "God helps them who help themselves."

God gives us the answers, but if the answers don't line up with the teachings of the "club", the church, you belong to, then it's back to square one. We're told the Bible was interpreted incorrectly.

She's told she didn't pray hard enough.

When people get married to fulfill the church's doctrine, this is not "made by God". It's a sham; it adds to the dissension, encourages suffocating the hidden anger, the need to "get even" with society.

Jesus gave an evasive, rhetorical answer to the question about marriage. That was then; now we need to update the concept for better results, less divorce and violent treatment of wives and unwanted children. That might work...?

It is apparent then, with the complexities of marriage, the added difficulty and stress of having children is too much for some people in the inner city. This struggle for existence can cause someone to crack, explode in anger and frustration.

Maybe we should listen to how people feel about marriage - take them seriously!

Watch what they do and what they say. Take them *seriously*!

*I know two men who said they want to get married. But, somehow every girl they've met doesn't qualify.*

*I asked the men what the problem was with the young ladies.*

*One girl was too young (8 years younger). One girl was too small (short). One girl was - "Oh, I don't know...." and so on.*

*One guy was silent and looked off into the horizon...*

*Are they serious about marriage?*

*Leave them alone.*

# LGBTQ

Lesbians, Gays, Bisexuals, Transgenders, Queers are all human beings, nothing more, nothing less.

Whether you like it or not, God made them male and female, man and woman.

But they don't chose to be "labeled," "boxed in" to one gender. They don't "feel" right under that label.

So they are condemned, ridiculed, tortured and killed because we, Christians, believe these people are not "Godly", nor following scripture.

We take judgement and reparation in our own hands. So, we do the "Christian" thing and condemn them, kill them at times, ostracize them - that'll teach them about Christian love!

How dare we!

This is God's domain, let God take care of it. Our job, as Christians is to show them Love, mercy and acceptance. - unless of course they're not in my corner of Christianity - if only they'd convert, then I could accept them!

How do you think they feel at being ridiculed, tormented, hounded, cursed...? You don't like them? You don't accept them - fine, you don't have to.

But, what **you have to do, is leave them to God**, *"you, who are you to judge your neighbor?"*
James 4:12

They say they *feel like a woman*, they *feel like a man…*

I have no idea what it *feels like* to be a woman, other than what I feel. I can't tell you what I feel, because I have never felt anything else. I am very limited in my knowledge of what it feels like to be something else.

Perhaps *feeling* like something is only an opinion…?

When we condemn these people from the pulpit, or from a place of smug security, we are absolutely out of place commenting on the *feelings* of others.

Jesus came purposefully, to get us away from judging others unfairly, judging out of ignorance and judging even ourself.

But yet, we are required to judge when we see or do wrong action, action against others. If someone wants to wear a disguise of Batman, Superman, Wonder Woman, and they obviously aren't, let go of it. We have no way of knowing what's on someone's mind.

Maybe they really believe they're a woman, or a man, what's that to us?

That scripture comes from the OLD Testament. You cannot live in the OLD Testament and the NEW at the same time. They contradict each other. And that's the point - God sent Jesus to teach us a better understanding of what His Father had in mind.

## "EENY MEENY MINY MO…"

As Christians many of us throw out the baby with the bath water. We pick out one, or two, beliefs from another Christian religion and say how wrong it is. We say that denomination is wrong because they believe such and such.

Instead of being grateful we're "Christians", we divide ourselves into private clubs; we are suspect of the other denominations, they're not going to be admitted into the Pearly Gates, we say.

On one occasion a student in my Public Speaking Class gave a speech on the wrongs of some Christian beliefs and extolled her own. The student said that it is a common belief Catholics worship idols -

**They do not!**

The student said Catholics pray to statues and holy pictures.

**They do not!**

I will ask that student of he or she has any pictures of their family, friends or special people in their wallet. Almost always they'll pull up some photos of their boy friend, best friend, Justin Bieber, Googoo, their pet dog and I'll say, "Oh so these are the idols you worship. You have their image in your wallet and you smile when you look at them and think about the fun times - these are your idols."

No, they're not idols to worship. They're a reminder of people, places where everyone had a good time; everyone was happy, loved and secure in that moment. Statues, holy pictures are just that, inanimate objects to remind you you're loved and cared for.

I tell my students, "I don't care who, or what, you don't like. But don't like it on the correct terminology - get it right. Don't dislike something on the wrong information."

Find out for yourself, go to the *source* and learn the truth.

And, yes, you can pray directly to God, no "interventions" are necessary. Or, you can pray to a tree, a stone… it's the intent that God hears; He hears what's in your heart. You don't need to bow to the East at morning, nor spin three times to your left at night while holding a sprig of sesame seeds.

God does not care HOW you worship, He hears your INTENT.

If God doesn't care how you worship Him, why should you care how others worship Him?

We Christians often make a private club out of our tabernacles. You need a password to get in, or better yet, a 20 dollar bill. One organization has a secret handshake to get in - like a boys' hide-out up in a tree.

Tiresome. Immature.

As Christians, our only concern is to correct the obvious wrongs against humanity: war, incest, abuse, robbery, murder… poverty, despair, ignorance, unwanted children, scamming people, ridiculing someone…cheating people in their salaries, pensions - correcting those wrongs is our job.

Also it's unethical to hire people of your belief system and cut out others who are perhaps more qualified.

We need to send missionaries into the dark, secret passages of the inner city, into the hidden lairs of the Anti Christ and open the windows of knowledge - bring in the Light.

Are we doing it? Are YOU doing it?

Let's review the …

**PREAMBLE**…(to the Constitution)

"We the People of the United States, in Order to form a more perfect Union, establish Justice, insure domestic Tranquility, provide for the common defence, promote the general Welfare, and secure the Blessings of Liberty to ourselves and our Posterity, do ordain and establish this Constitution for the United States of America."

So, at this point in our nation, what have we done to

**establish Justice?** - *for all?*

So, at this point in our nation, what have we done to

**provide for the common defense?**

So, at this point in our nation, what have we done to

**insure domestic Tranquility?** - *in the inner city?*

So, at this point in our nation, what have we done to

**promote the general Welfare?** - *in the inner city?*

So, at this point in our nation, what have we done to

**secure the Blessings of Liberty** - *for all?*

For these answers look at the media, look at the news, look at the state of our nation, look at the crime rate, look at the gratuitous violence, school shootings, drugs rampant in our schools, the divorce rate, the division of peoples in neighborhoods, the division among churches, beliefs.

The increase acquisition and support of "non profit charities", the melee of our political system. Liars, cheats and thieves, womanizers and buffoons are in charge.

# PARENTING

It seems many parents are afraid to say, "No." They don't want to be "unfair," to "not understand" their children. The parent want to be "cool."

*My daughter, 18, just out of high school, announced to me she and her girl friend were going to hitch-hike to Oregon for the summer. We lived in San Francisco.*

*She stood in front of me, face to face, and announced, "Teena and I are going to hitch hike to Oregon this summer." I looked into her beautiful face framed by long, silky golden hair and said, "No, you're not." There was no discussion. End of discussion.*

Of course she was upset, she hurled herself on the couch, in tears,

"This is my only chance at happiness!"

I thought, "Probably not."

It wasn't.

Parents seem to feel the word, "No," will destroy their child's psyche, their creativity, their self image, their future perceptions of Life - no, it won't.

The word, "NO", is a fence, a wall, that surrounds something of value. A "fence" limits freedom, a fence is a restraint. Some times a fence shuts out the sunlight and sometimes it can lock you in with an enemy - or, a friend.

But, the real purpose of a fence is to keep someone safe, secure. It is a barrier so no one will get lost, not get attacked. Usually a fence has a strong gate that shuts and opens and may have a lock. The gate should not blow freely in the wind.

The gate, the message of "No," should be, "You are my responsibility. I brought you in to this world out of Love, I love you. I will not allow anything or anyone harm you. I see harm in this decision of yours; let's discuss what I understand and I want to hear how you understand the situation."

That "fence" has a gate, you open the gate and say, "Let's discuss this…" The "gate" can swing freely letting ideas flow in both directions.

So, discuss what you "see," then listen to a *rational* counter-argument - and, by the way, since I am a Communications Instructor, let me explain that the word, "argument" simply means "*opinion*, point of view" - NOT a quarrel, a verbal fight. A "quarrel" or verbal "fight" is counter productive, a waste of energy and Love.

You, as the parent give your "argument", your point of view. The the other person gives their point of view - their "argument."

And you each LISTEN to what is being said, what is the *real* message? Is it the issue at hand, or some underlying fear? It might even be a good idea to ask, "What did I just say?" or "What did you just say?"

Maybe the person heard something entirely different from what you thought you said. That is always a strong possibility.

Sincere communication is essential and healthy.

# CHRISTIAN POTPOURRI

How many denominations are there?

I chose the better known Christian organizations as we all look to Him as our Savior, the One, the Son of God who gave His life to give us Everlasting Life.

*Basic beliefs of most Christian organizations are:*

*Amish: Jesus Christ is God's Son, died on the cross for our sins*

*Assembly of God: Christ is Savior and Lord*

*Baptists: Jesus Christ is Lord and Savior*

*First Baptists: The Gospel Message of Jesus Christ is the most important message in all of history*

*Catholic (Roman): The Resurrection of Jesus and forgiveness of sins*

*Christian Science: Acknowledge Jesus as the Son of God*

*Episcopalian (Anglican): Jesus is the Son of God*

*Four Square: Jesus is King and Savior*

*Jehovah's Witnesses: Jesus is our Savior and Son of God*

*Lutherans: Humans are saved by God's grace*

*Messianic Jews: Jesus is the Messiah*

*Methodists: The Divinity of Jesus*

*Orthodox: God revealed Himself in Jesus Christ*

97

*Pentecostal: Salvation through Jesus*

*Quakers: A belief in Christian Ideals*

*Salvation Army: Jesus atones for the sins of the world*

*Seventh Day Adventists: Salvation comes through faith in Jesus Christ*

*Unitarianism: Jesus is the model for one's own life*

## WHERE CHRISTIANS AGREE

Among the Christian religions is the belief that Jesus is the *only* Son of God. He will keep his promise to return and save our souls. He is the Savior of Mankind and only through Him can we all be saved from eternal darkness.

Perhaps in our goal to lift people out of darkness into the light, we might want to base our efforts on the teachings in the New Testament.

Jesus came to enlighten us and walk with us out of ignorance in the way of Peace, Love and Acceptance of all peoples.

## WHERE CHRISTIANS DON'T AGREE

We may not agree on what day we should observe the Sabbath. We may not agree on Friday, Saturday or Sunday.

Does that really matter?

We may not agree on water or wine at communion.

Does that really matter?

We will most definitely not agree on abortion, birth control, gay rights and women's rights. Perhaps one day these disagreements can be cleared up so people will approach their lives in a way Fundamental Christians would better understand.

These issues are NOT insurmountable.

**Abortion** is a serious issue within all Christian assemblies. Perhaps if we eliminate the *need for abortion* - rape, unwanted babies, babies conceived out of ignorance, immaturity and psychological disturbances, the issue of abortion would be solved.

Every child should be wanted and loved. It's the task of Christians to see this is a reality.

**Women's Rights**: Christians, stop squabbling about a woman's place is under her husband's rule and she should keep silent. Our concern is not specifically about controlling women. We all need to focus on lifting the Lost souls of the Inner City up to self respect.

Maybe we should listen to women and take their issues seriously - Jesus did.

One serious issue I, as a woman, have with Fundamentalist teachings toward women, is when we have an on-going problem that is eating at our soul, we're told, "Take it to the Lord in payer - turn it over to Jesus."

We do. But, the problem continues. Then, we're told, "You didn't try hard enough. You didn't turn it over good enough, soon enough, sincere enough…"

If we pray for help to change our husband - he beats me, he abuses me, he cheats… We're told you must try harder.

In other words, we lose. We lose because the problem persists and we lose because we can't pray hard enough to remove the problem - it's our fault. We are condemned coming or going.

**Gays:** Christians can stop squabbling about gays, abominations and the like; we can leave them to God for their salvation - wouldn't that make more sense than condemning them? Is condemning *anyone* the right of a Christian?

Those issues are not a part of our teaching people self-respect through education, self pride through personal achievement. Understanding the use of the law, the purpose of the law, respect for society in general.

If we are going to save America from the decadence, increasing violence, exponential departures from God, the increasing insults to God, we **ALL** have to **UNITE** in our inner strength, our belief in the teachings of Jesus, and follow his example.

**ALL** Christians must "Go and do likewise", teach people the Way, the Light. Teach people their value, show them how to live life the fullest in the teachings of the Savior. Show them how gifted they are and how to live in self pride through the examples of Jesus.

Feeling sorry for people is unproductive. Sometimes when a wound needs attention, the cure can be painful. Maybe it's not healing under the bandages and the treatment is painful to fix.

In the medical profession the healer has to steel himself against the bitterness of the patient's anger, lashing out because of pain. The patient can't see the healing thing place, it's all a matter of faith. But the healer is held responsible for the suffering.

And, we can't expect people, confused, walking in darkness to find the Light on their own. They have to be shown, be taught, how to walk a clean, joy-full path in their rightful place in society.

# GOD IS NOT A GOOD LUCK CHARM

Self determinism may seem like anti-God, it's not. But all too often we use God as a talisman, some "thing" to ward off evil, a good luck charm.

*I was sitting on a bus next to a college girl. We were talking about God. She showed me her scapular, a square cloth religious icon worn on a string around the neck.*

*She explained, "The priest said as long as I have this on, God will protect me."*

*I commented, "God is not in a piece of cloth. God is always with you, always cares about you. You are loved."*

*There's a belief system that puts faith in wearing secret underwear...?*

**ONWARD CHRISTIAN SOLDIERS** marching as to war...

When one of our young people join the military in service of our country, they are obliged to swear allegiance to defend our Constitution:

> I, _____, do solemnly swear (or affirm) that I will support and defend the Constitution of the United States *against all enemies, foreign* and domestic; that I will bear true faith and allegiance to the same...

Are we Christians defending America **against all enemies, foreign...?**

Or, do we persist to insist we're "all alike..."?

**NO, we're not!**

**Read - all of their literature.**

**Do we defend:**

The serpent in the inner cities, encouraging dissension in the prisons, pushing drugs on our children, in our government, riddled with greed, lies, mental poison…

Are our schools teaching lies about the Constitution and Christianity?

Christians, our mission is to go into these areas, clean up the mess of the serpent. This is God's country and we are God's children.

## PITY, OR GUIDANCE?

When we Christians march into the inner cities of the high-crime neighborhoods, will we feel sorry for the people there, or will we teach them acceptable behaviors from the start?

Feeling sorry for anyone is an insult. Teach them to live a better life.

Do we look down on the disadvantaged with a "so sorry what has happened to you" look, or reach out and treat them as though they have hope..?

# FREE WILL OR DETERMINISM

The Bible teaches:

Ask, and it shall be given unto you.

Seek and ye shall find.

Knock and it will be opened unto you

If you want help from God, guidance, spiritual enrichment, self-growth, understanding, inner strength, it's there - just reach out and help yourself. But, God demands your cooperation. God will give you what is *right for you*, but you have to actively *seek it out*; you have to *ask for it - be ready,* and then, *go get it - it's there!*

*This advice would imply free will.*

We're being told, you can have something, just tell me what you want. But, it's as though we stand in front of a buffet God has set out for us and, we stand, staring at cabbage and carrots trying to make up our mind what we want.

*I have actually been in buffets where one woman would hold up the line by trying to decide which slice of tomato to take! So-o annoying!*

Can you imagine God having a choice of directions, of jobs, of solving dilemmas that can all be given to you, if you just snap out

103

of your daze and choose! God will not make your choices for you! That's your job!

And, we're told by friends, that to want something, to ask God for favors, is selfish. Did God say that? Did God set out a whole chocolate cake in front of you and say,"This is all for you, but you can have only one bite"?

No, the whole thing is yours, but, be careful, you might get sick on it.

God will not deny the smallest request. We're told that even a sparrow, a tiny, homely bird can make its home in the corner of God's altar.

Nothing is too small, unimportant, for God. He's not far away - He can be reached and touched.

"Yea, the sparrow has found him a house, and the swallow a nest for herself, where she may lay her young, even your altars, O LORD of hosts, my King, and my God." Psalm 84:3

God never turns away from us, but, out of ignorance we sometimes turn away from Him.

When someone is lost, as those people are who live in high crime areas, how can they know where to go for change, for help, for best guidance…?

To give them help, there's no time or place that's required for God - they can ask, right where they're standing. God will hear them. *God will answer.*

## *But we Christians have to turn on the Light for them to see clearly.*

Assuming we can get Christian denominations united to work together toward the common goal of lifting America out of the slew of ignorance and violence, like the Trojan horse, we need to be alert for people disguised as Christians to cancel the good we may have done.

We must be vigilant and focus on the work at hand.

**IGNORANCE**

When I was a child in the first grade, I knew nothing about arithmetic and the totals of columns were often wrong. Instead of blaming the numbers for being wrong, the nuns had me do the problem over and explained how to get the right total - it was my error due to my ignorance.

Instead of feeling "sorry" for "disadvantaged" people we need to have them understand they're largely responsible for their own incorrect calculations, their own ignorance, and how to fix them.

Just because you don't know something is no excuse not to learn it, and do it right, no matter how many tries it takes.

This is why Christian denominations must join forces, go into the dark ignorance of the inner city and bring the Light, education, enlightenment, self-awareness, self respect to those who walk in darkness.

We have to combine forces to teach people, as Jesus did, how to understand that they can uplift their own life by changing the way they live it, change their understanding of the negative past behavior and understand the path of Light is the only path.

In particular, the young women must be taught to understand self-respect, not to allow themselves to be used to satisfy some man's ego.

Only through education can one achieve understanding of the value of self, how to respect one's self and others. We have control over our lives to some degree. We can help make it good, or we can let others control us and make our life bad.

## *"DEMON"*-I-ZATIONS

Let's look at "denominations" more closely. What I have observed is each group of Christians is a closed club, and have members, often with closed minds.

*At my church, Episcopalian, I was asked to take charge of a woman from another state. Her son was dying of Aids in a local hospice.*

*She needed chauffeuring, lodging, dining, in general, plus everything getting what we could for the comfort of her son.*

*We all chipped in to help her out even though she was not Episcopalian - we had no concern about that. For several weeks, I had about 80% of her care. I had no problem with that.*

*One day I took off work purposely to drive her to her appointments and shopping.*

*In the car she told me she had joined the Mormon organization - they told her that they had the one true God and all Episcopalians are boozers and queers.*

*If the denominations mud-sling at each other - "demon" -izing each other, not only is the solidarity of America lost, Jesus is buried in the mud slide.*

*I didn't point out that no Mormon had taken a day off work to chauffeur her around. She was in the car with a boozer or queer - of which I am neither.*

*When I dropped her off I chose not to see her again.*

# DON'T PROSELYTIZE IN GREEK

Don't talk your religious lingo to someone who is living in the depths of Dante's Inferno. For people who have never felt love, who have never felt acceptance, babbling something about love, forgiveness, acceptance, sins, won't mean much. It all sounds like Greek to the uninitiated.

I've mentioned before, my stepfather made my life Hell. I spent my young years, running, hiding, on guard, suspicious, alert, ever looking over my shoulder.

I rarely stayed home. We lived in the country so I'd go into the forest or sleep on the rolling hills with my dog. Anything to stay out of the house.

I was a wild child. Thank God I lived in the country. The space, the sun, the towering trees, fresh breezes, floating clouds of angels, all were uplifting moments of pleasure. I was not alone. I talked to the manzanita, the dandelions, my dog, God.

One day the pastor's wife invited me for tea. Why? Why was someone being nice to *me?* What was she up to...?

To this day I can feel fear, what was she going to do to me - what was she up to?

Sometimes I sit and cry for that lonely, lost child. "How lucky to be aborted," I thought.

Mother mentioned several times in my youth, that I wasn't wanted, she had several abortions, but I didn't abort. She had wanted a son and even had a boy's name picked out, Antonio. One of my cousin's named me Carolyn after her dance teacher. And my father even put down the wrong name on my birth certificate - he and mother never even discussed it.

I was sad I was here, unwanted, unloved. But to this day I understand there are times when abortion is welcome, it can be a far better choice than Life.

The pastor's wife was sweet. She gently asked me, "How are things at home?"

Are you kidding! No way would I ever tell anyone!

I sat on the edge of the chair, "Fine!" I snapped, "You'll never get anything out of me," I thought.

She didn't.

As I grew older, I took revenge on everyone around me. I made them suffer because I was suffering. I got even with them for not being wanted, not being loved and not being a boy.

I had an acerbic wit; a relentless ability to copy, imitate, single out fears and flaws in others, magnify them and ridicule them, make fun of them, particularly boys. I hit them with a blinding fury that caught them off guard. Oh, boy! Did I get even!!

I especially hated girls who had a father who loved them, a mother who listened to them and answered appropriately, who had a home, a room of their own, who looked forward to going home after school, who didn't cling to their dog for love, my heart ached for the love they had.

Today, I am sorry I hurt people, so unnecessary. I try to make amends as I can.

At this moment my housekeeper just finished cleaning my house, 5 straight hours and the place looks gorgeous. Now what's she going to do? It's 3:00 pm - she's going to take her young son to the park. How wonderful! She loves him!

I wish everyone could have such an experience.

So talking words of salvation, Jesus loves you, comfort, turn to God in prayer, blah, blah, blah. The biggest laugh I had as a child was when someone said, "You're loved..."

I thought, "Prove it."

People who walk in darkness don't hear words, they don't see, they can only feel. People in the inner cities don't see the Light for the shadows, the formless shadows that lead them deeper into darkness.

Well, eventually "love" was proved to me. But not by words, by simple kindnesses, acts of silent devotion that burned the hate in my mind and filled my heart with Light.

Love, acceptance, have to be shown, demonstrated, not explained. Patience, Charity, as it says in 1st Corinthians, 13th chapter, is the only way to teach, to save someone. When people are lost, they have to be led to safety, not only by words, but by patience and demonstration.

Let them lead you to their place of darkness and then show them the Light, it's there; they may have to look hard, but there is always the Light in the darkness.

Only we, Christians, can lift up this nation to be the spiritual one God created it to be. Is there oil in your lamp?

# CHRISTIANS, WHERE IN HELL ARE YOU?

Only Christians can stop this evil! So, where in Hell are you!!

WHAT are you thinking?

"My daddy was a Free Methodist and his father before him - if it's good enough for them - it's good enough for me."

"All my relatives are Four Square and so am I. I see no need to change."

"It's a venial sin not to be a Catholic, the priest said so."

"Hallelujah! Praise the Lord, we are Baptists, saved by the blood of Jesus!"

So, does this mean we stand alone in groups, to fight the Anti Christ? The forces of Evil that surrounds us all **here** and even **now** are the challenge only for Jehovah's Witnesses?

Isn't this challenge between good and evil forces - *heaven and earth, salvation* - *the prize of **eternal** salvation* - important enough to put on the whole armor of God, and as a **united army** go forth to fight for Jesus, the Son of God?

Jesus said, "When two or more are gathered in my name, there I am in the midst of them…"

We Christians don't need a church - four walls and air conditioning. All we need is YOU and ME, and and HER and HIM and THEM over there…

UNITE as ONE BODY in CHRIST

The Anti Christ is hot on our heels and we bicker about wine or grape juice, bread or wafers, hymns or not, bonnets or not, baptism or not - do you see how ridiculous this nonsense is in the wake **of anti-Christian** forces waiting in the wings, stepping on our heels?

## A HOUSE DIVIDED AGAINST ITSELF CAN NOT STAND

*The night is coming…*

## CHRISTIANS WHERE DO WE GO FROM HERE? Are we "Christians," or "denominations?"

God is indescribable, personal, but religion is man-made. It's when society agrees on a specific course of life. God is indifferent to what we choose, the choice is ours. We interpret the Bible according to our personal will.

If you're a Christian you live by the teachings of the New Testament, you *follow Jesus.*

## Whatever Jesus did,

## <u>you do.</u>

Have you noticed, the word itself, 'Christian', has the word, "Christ" imbedded in it. You cannot have the concept of "Christ" in your beliefs and follow the ancient teachings. That's why we have the **NEW** Testament.

When in doubt, ask Jesus, go to His words and listen carefully.

When we Christians go into Chicago, Detroit, Washington, D.C., Atlanta, teach people in the language they know. Teach them violence is not productive - it works against them. Teach them that bringing a child into this world is a huge responsibility and show them the difficulties required in that life-changing task. Ask them, "Are you ready for the stress, dedication and relentless pressure of the care and responsibility of another life?"

Show the unloved, the angry, hurt souls, the tattoo-covered, body pierced, head-shaved, drugged out unwanted thousands of lost souls how they can build a better world for themselves. Teach them how to love themselves, respect themselves. Show them they don't have to destroy others to stop their own pain of rejection.

Don't criticize their destructive way of life, show them a better way. That's what Jesus did, the woman at the well. He didn't criticize her, he loved her.

Don't let them blame society, the police, the "haves" - lack of home life is the reason for choosing the wrong path, a path that leads to an empty life.

That's all these violent souls need, love, unconditional love. As Christians we must unite, on the "battle field". We must stop nit-picking about the Sabbath was the 6th day, the 7th day… Does God have a calendar with the days of the week marked off?

*Every day is the Sabbath day.*

Placating, appeasing or feeling sorry for people in need of help, of change, is definitely NOT the way to go. You don't teach people by petting their bruises, calling them "deprived", "downtrodden", "disadvantaged", "poor things" - this attitude is demeaning, self defeating and insulting.

## REWARD AND PUNISHMENT

Go back to Psych 101, Henry James, reward and punishment. When someone does well, you reward them. When someone messes up, they fix it until it's right. Then, when it's done right, you reward them.

The inner city population early understands reward and punishment. It is the known, their life story.

You explain, clearly, intelligently, why things are done the way they are, maybe in both societies, mainstream and "dis" advantaged.

Carefully consider their input. Lead them into the direction of better choices. Tell them "why," things are a certain way. The terminology may be far above their comprehension. Talk in their own language.

Learn their language, teach them how to respect authority, even when it's wrong. Help them to understand the behavior of the past, the negativity builds up over years of poor choices affect the presses and the future. Teach them how to build up a reputation of self-respect built on understanding the value in mainstream society.

Teach them the value and dignity of developing self control over impulses. We are not creatures of happenstance, we can order our lives, we have self determination.

# CHRISTIAN SOLDIERS, UNITE! PUT ON THE WHOLE ARMOR OF GOD!

## <u>Now</u> is the time!

**Recommended readings:**

**The New Testament**

The Koran

"Born Again," Charles Colson

"Mr. God, this is Anna" Finn

The Book of Mormon

"Unspeakable" by Chris Hedges

"Autobiography of a Recovering Skinhead" Frank Meeink

The poem "Invictus", Wm Henley

# ABOUT THE AUTHOR

**Carolyn Franklin**

Carolyn Franklin: Instructor: Communication Studies M.A., Education M. A., Psychology B. A. San Francisco Opera, Voice Coach, Lecturer

voicedynamicscf@yahoo.com

# PUBLICATIONS BY
# CAROLYN FRANKLIN M. A.

*Adam, First Man or First Mouse?*

*Athena: Goddess of Communication Strategies*

*Attorneys: The art of public speaking*

*Christians, where in Hell are you?*

*Communication Strategies for Successful Women*

*Coping With Bullies: A gentle approach*

*Do You Have Thinky Thoughts, Too?*

*E-Z Dictionary*

*How to talk to Texans and Other Foreigners*

*Increase Your Emotional Intelligence*

*Just Be Yourself Whoever That Is*

*#Metoo, Now, Women's Lib, Just Say No: Why they'll never work*

*Police Brutality+Crime+Welfare = Birth Control*

*The Princess and the Pee: Caring for a Special Needs Person*

*Recipes From My Neapolitan Family: A love story*

*Rhetoric and Public Speaking*

*The Story of Mary: Miracles, mayhem and mirth*

*Your Voice Your Personality*

*Welfare + Diversity = Social Sucide*

*Women at Work: Win-win communication strategies*

*Women Bullying Women: An effect of Women's Lib*